Biblical
ISRAEL

Biblical ISRAEL

A People's History

Jorge Pixley

Fortress Press, Minneapolis

BIBLICAL HISTORY
A People's History

Cover art "Lachish" by Sandra Bowden

Cover design by Lecy Design
Interior design and graphics by McCormick Creative

Pixley, Jorge V.
[Historia sagrada, historia popular. English]
Biblical Israel : a people's history / Jorge Pixley.
p. cm.
Includes bibliographical references and index.
ISBN 0-8006-2551-X :
1. Jews—History—To 70 A.D. 2. Judaism—History—To 70 A.D.
3. Bible. O.T.—History of Biblical events. I. Title.
DS117.P56 1992
933—dc20 92-38146
CIP

The paper used in this publication meets the minimum requirements of American National Standard for Information Sciences—Permanence of Paper for Printed Library Materials, ANSI Z329.48-1984. ∞™

Manufactured in the U.S.A. 1–2551

96 95 94 93 92 1 2 3 4 5 6 7 8 9 10

Contents

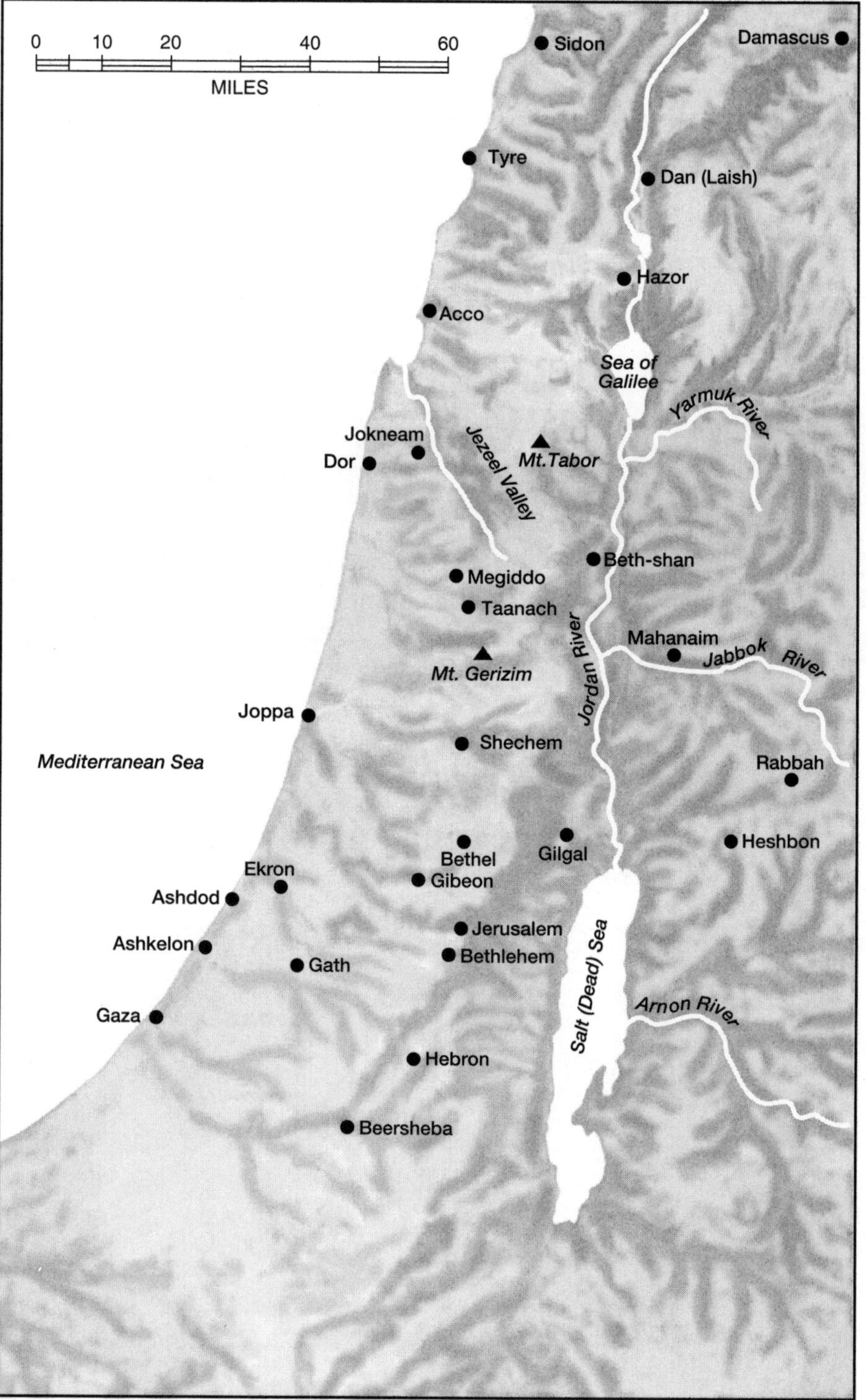
0
10
20
40
60
MILES
Sidon
Damascus
Tyre
Dan (Laish)
Hazor
Acco
Sea of Galilee
Yarmuk River
Jokneam
Dor
Jezeel Valley
Mt.Tabor
Beth-shan
Megiddo
Taanach
Jordan River
Mahanaim
Jabbok River
Mt. Gerizim
Joppa
Shechem
Mediterranean Sea
Rabbah
Bethel
Gilgal
Heshbon
Ekron
Gibeon
Ashdod
Jerusalem
Ashkelon
Gath
Bethlehem
Salt (Dead) Sea
Gaza
Arnon River
Hebron
Beersheba

Preface

This book presents a brief history of Israel during the biblical period. Biblical Israel is defined by the following measures: (1) Chronologically, this period extends from Moses to Simon bar Cosiba, approximately 1220 B.C.E. to 135 C.E., excluding the patriarchal antecedents of Israel, on the one hand, and the derivation of this history in the Christian church and Rabbinic Judaism, on the other hand. (2) Geographically, this history is limited by the confines of the land of Canaan or Palestine, two names for the same land situated between the Mediterranean Sea on the west, the desert to the east and the south, and the Lebanese mountains to the north, excluding, therefore, the stories of the ancient related Jewish groups that lived outside this land, in Babylon, Egypt, Persia, and other places. (3) Sociologically, Israel during those thirteen hundred years was the project of a peasant nation that struggled to survive and to give itself the structures necessary for its survival.

This definition of biblical Israel is by no means obvious. The development of the history will serve as its justification, in the measure in which it is able to account for the documents (mostly biblical) and for the archaeological remains better than alternative parameters can.

The author of this book is a professor of Bible in a Christian (Baptist) theological seminary. This history is written for seminarians, students, pastors, Sunday school teachers, and delegates of the Word. It proposes to offer a historical framework for reading with greater understanding the sacred books to persons who have a basic knowledge of the biblical books and a faith in the God of the Bible. For this reason we devote much space to situating the biblical books historically and sociologically, much more space than would be strictly necessary in a history of Israel that was religiously disinterested. It is our conviction, however, that understanding the history of Israel is also useful, even valuable, for those who are not believers. It is a history peculiarly transparent to the depths of the human condition, to which we have remarkably perceptive testimonies in the Bible. The author believes he has written a book that can be read with profit and without offense by those who do not believe in the providence of God in human history.

The pedagogical intentions of this work impose criteria of simplicity and brevity. Scholars still debate many topics that are here presented without the scholarly justification that would be required in a work addressed to historians of Israel. The Bibliography therefore functions both to lead readers to more comprehensive resources and to alert teachers and biblical critics to our more important and gratefully acknowledged scholarly debts.

Managua, Nicaragua —*Jorge Pixley*

1
Interpretive Keys

We wish to understand the meaning of the events of the history of Israel, but meaning in history does not lie on the surface of its events ready to be read by the naked and untrained eye. To discover the meaning of historical events we must explore beneath the surface. In the documents left behind in any history special interests can conceal the meaning of the flow of events. In these circumstances the search for meaning often takes on the characteristics of detective work. The history of Israel is no exception to these problems. The books that make up our Bible, which are the main documents for the history of Israel, also reflect the work of concealment to which we refer.

This being the case, we need keys to interpret the texts, much like codes used to decipher a cryptic message. We propose two keys, one theological and one sociological.

A theological key, the Exodus. The exodus from slavery in Egypt is not an event like any other within the history of Israel. It is the founding event of the people of Israel. A nation is constituted by its founding event or events. The British colonies in America made their independence a very self-conscious foundation inscribed in words and institutions through a constitution that created a nation of free property owners; the United States has never escaped from this way of being. Haiti was founded by a long and difficult slave revolt of Africans in America, and even its most tyrannical rulers have not been able to escape its nature as a nation of blacks who gained freedom by successfully fighting whites.

In the case of Israel, history was counted from the Exodus (1 Kings 6:1, Deut. 9:7, Judg. 19:30, Jer. 7:25, and so on), but it meant much more. It meant that for Israel the Exodus was a revelatory event. Israel will know God as Yahweh, the God who brought them out of bondage: "I, Yahweh, am your God, who brought you up out of Egypt, out of the house of bondage" (Exod. 20:2; cf. also Hos. 11:1; 12:10; 13:4; Deut. 6:12; 13:6; Judg. 2:1; 1 Kings 12:28, and others). Now, "God" is a very slippery word, which has been used and continues to be used in a deceptive manner to refer to the "same" Creator and Supreme Being conceived in quite diverse ways. In Israel, its correct referent is always that God who redeemed Israel from slavery in Egypt. Any god who is not the savior of the poor and oppressed cannot be the true God of Israel.

We will use this key to unmask ideological language within the biblical texts. A god who legitimates the oppression of peasants, no matter how solemn its cult, is not the true God of Israel, for the true God is only that One who hears the cries of the oppressed and frees them from their oppressors.

A sociological key: the "Asiatic" or tributary mode of production. In the confessional ritual pronounced when the (male) Israelite brought the first fruits of his harvest to offer them to Yahweh, he recognized that Israel was a people that had been liberated from slavery and oppression by Yahweh (Deut. 26:6-9). This awareness of being a poor and oppressed people who struggle for life with the help of Yahweh is basic. Yahweh is the true God who hears the cries of those who are oppressed and Israel is the people of Yahweh that depends on Yahweh for the success of its struggles for liberation.

To identify those who were oppressed in the societies of ancient Palestine it is necessary to understand the dynamics that sustained those societies. During the long centuries of Israel's history many social configurations existed, but all of them were variations on one basic scheme whose structure must be understood at the outset.

We find in Genesis a simple description of this type of society, which prevailed throughout the ancient Near East (Gen. 47:13-25), with reference specifically to Egypt. We shall represent graphically the social relations of Egypt in a simple sketch:

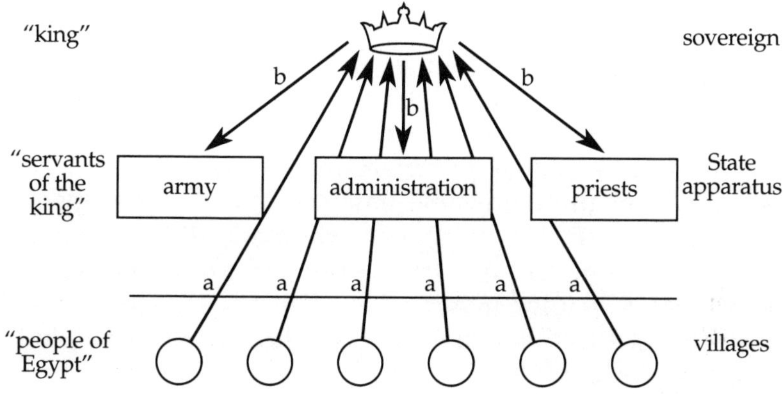

Diagram 1

Exodus frequently refers to Egyptian society with a list of three elements; the king, the servants of the king, and the people (for example, Exod 9:14). Let us look at each of these elements, which made up all the societies of the Ancient Near East, not just Egyptian society.

The people referred to the peasant mass, comprising the bulk of the population. They lived in small villages, represented in the diagram by the circles at the base. The villages were the productive units of the society (and not family farms, as in old Germanic society, or factories as in nineteenth-century England, or *fazendas*, "plantations" as in nineteenth-century Brazil, for instance). Each village was more or less autonomous, producing what it required to meet its needs. It had only slight contacts with other villages. In the surrounding fields each village cultivated its basic grains and raised animals to satisfy the need for milk and wool. Ideologically, the village expressed its unity in terms of a common lineage, descent from a common ancestor. The internal government of the village was in the hands of a council of "elders," the heads of its families. The lands of the village were usually village property. They were assigned by the elders to the village families in accordance with the capacity of each to work them, and were redistributed as families grew or languished. The daily routine for field workers was to leave the village at the crack of dawn to accomplish what needed to be done in fields that might be a walk of an hour or two away.

The king of Egypt was the titular owner of all the land, all the animals, and all the persons of the country. It is obvious that no single person could exercise effective possession over the lands, the animals, and the persons of the country. His title of property was made effective in real terms in that he was due tribute from all and every village of the land (arrows marked *a* in diagram 1). The tribute was charged to the village and not directly to its families or its individuals.

Tribute was charged on the produce of the land, a fifth of what was collected, according to the Genesis account. This surely varied from place to place and time to time, but each village was obligated to pay such tribute. Some similar system would have been levied on the animals and the products of local skilled-craft work. Tribute was also imposed in the form of labor upon each village. Quotas of labor were assessed for the tasks of the kingdom, both those that might seem to us of public utility, such as the maintenance required for dikes and irrigation ditches, and what seems sumptuary, like temples, monuments, and palaces.

During the term of a wise king, the system provided a fairly stable exchange with mutual benefits. In exchange for the exacted tribute the king provided the protection of his army and the benefits of hydraulic works to control floods and provide irrigation, roads adequate for moving goods, and the worthy celebration of national festivities. Nevertheless, because the king had a monopoly on real power, the system allowed for crass abuses in the hands of an unwise or tyrannical ruler.

The servants of the king were persons directly dependent on the crown who carried out the will of the king in various spheres of national life. They served at the will or the whim of the king, and received their provisions from the king's treasury in exchange (arrows marked *b* in diagram 1). To assure the stability of the kingdom it would be necessary to maintain a strong army to defend the state against dangers from within and without the nation. The officials of the army served at the pleasure of the king and the king was the commander-in-chief. Because military personnel would lose their village ties in the course of their duties, it seems correct to assume that military life was usually hereditary and not based in villages but in cities, like the remainder of the state bureaucracy.

To collect and distribute the tribute of the villages the king required a large body of administrative officials. The civil administration of the kingdom would include accountants, watchmen, construction foremen, transportation personnel, scribes, and even ministers of state. All depended on the royal treasury for their sustenance and served at the pleasure of the king.

It is important to take into account the absolute necessity of a religious apparatus in this system (the *priests* in diagram 1). In this tributary society everybody was in one way or another a slave, with the sole exception of the king. Even the royal family was subject to the absolute will of the king. The king occupied a position in the society that was absolutely unique. In the daily experience of his subjects the king was a mortal god. He had the power of life and death over every person in the land. He held in his hands the disposal of all the wealth in the land. Nevertheless, his limitation—his mortality—revealed the fragility of his divine position and made a religious apparatus necessary to celebrate the greatness of the nation and within it the unique and indispensable role of its god-king. The religious apparatus within an "Asiatic" or tributary society was directly linked to the king by a strict logical necessity. Just as the king must be the commander-in-chief of the army, so he must also be the high priest who directs and controls religious activity in all of the realm. He needs prophets and theologians who will elaborate the theology to justify his absolute domination. He needs priests and rich temples to celebrate the festivals that confirm the system with great pomp.

All of the societies that enter into the history of biblical Israel can be understood as variants on this system of tributary societies, so the simple diagram we have examined in this chapter will serve as the sociological key to reading the Bible and the history of biblical Israel.

2
The Origins of Israel as a Nation of Tribes before 1400 B.C.E.

Pre-Israelite Canaan

We have marked 1220 B.C.E., the estimated date of the Exodus, as the date for the beginning of the history of Israel, but according to any theory about the origins of Israel—and there are three principal theories that we shall examine shortly—the ancestors of the tribes already lived in Canaan, or at least a goodly portion of those ancestors. It will, therefore, be helpful to examine the population of Palestine before the formation of Israel in the fourteenth century (from 1400 to 1300 B.C.E.).

We have two sources of knowledge about this period. On the one hand, excavations of the mounds left by ancient cities make it possible to estimate how many cities were inhabited during the century and how large their population was. The other source is a collection of letters from the Egyptian diplomatic office, letters that were discovered in the Egyptian location of Tel-el-amarna. Part of this diplomatic correspondence consists of exchanges with the kings of the city-states of Palestine, a region then under the control of the Egyptian Empire.

The most important fact revealed by these sources is that the population of Palestine was concentrated in the lower parts of the country, on the plain that borders the Mediterranean Sea and the Valley of Jezreel, which cuts through the central mountain chain from west to east at the level of Mount Carmel and the Sea of Galilee. These are the more fertile areas of the land, and they are also the areas through which the roads passed that were traveled by the caravans of merchants. The central chain of mountains, from north to south, is known successively as the mountains of Galilee, Ephraim, and Judah, which were then an area of forests and thickets, populated by wild animals, including lions. There were few cities in the mountains, the main ones in this period being from north to south, Hazor, Shechem, and Jerusalem. The map on page 7 attempts to represent this situation.

The Tel-el-amarna letters give an idea of the political situation in fourteenth century B.C.E. Palestine. The territory was divided up into many small kingdoms, each one around a city (for instance, Dor or Taanach), which controlled the surrounding villages and exacted tribute from them. Another source of income for the kings were the duties and tolls for passage imposed on merchants who traveled the roads that crossed the territory. All of these kings were subject to Egypt, to whom they in turn rendered tribute, but a constant state of conflict existed among them. Besides, all were plagued by the raids and uprisings of the *'apiru*, rebels of various sorts whose existence reflects the social discontent of the period.

Scientific Theories about the Emergence of Tribal Israel

Exegetes and biblical scholars have proposed three theories to explain the emergence of Israel as a league of tribes in the thirteenth century B.C.E. Before looking at them it is useful to point out that all recognize the diversity of elements that went into the formation of Israel and that, therefore, all of the theories contain a measure of truth. What is at stake is to decide which element can explain the unity of tribal Israel, which makes it necessary to choose among them. That is, the diversity inherent in a tribal system is obvious; it will continually threaten the unity of any tribal coalition. How can we explain the consciousness of unity that undoubtedly did exist among the tribes of Israel considering that as a federation of autonomous tribes Israel had no state to symbolize and impose unity and order?

1. The theory of a primitive racial unity. Some exegetes, among whom the late Yehezkel Kaufmann in Israel and John Bright in the United States stand out, consider that the ties of kinship among the tribes were sufficient to explain their unity. The Genesis stories about the patriarchs Abraham, Isaac, and Jacob presuppose a consciousness of kinship among the tribes, which are said in these sagas to descend from the twelve sons of Jacob (Genesis 30). Now, it is obvious when one reads the stories about the incorporation into Israel of the cities of Gibeon (Joshua 9), Shechem (Genesis 34) and Jerusalem (2 Samuel 5) that important elements within the tribes made no claim to have descended from the common trunk represented by Abraham. Nevertheless, these historians believe that it is possible to explain the national unity by means of the common kinship of large sectors of the tribes.

From the perspective of the poor, the apolitical nature of this theory raises suspicions. The "people of God" would have originated from a "natural" process that was not the result of human actions. The hostility between Israel and Canaan would then have to be explained as a racial conflict, humanly speaking, as we must in a history. Apart from the embarrassing fact that Israelites and Canaanites spoke the same language called "the tongue of Canaan" (Isaiah 19:18), this view makes the privileges of Israel as the people of God an arbitrary decision of Yahweh. On this view, the theological tendentiousness of which is evident, Yahweh will have heard the cries of the slaves in Egypt, not because they were unjustly oppressed but because they happened to be descendents of Abraham, Isaac, and Jacob. Exodus sometimes says this was the case, but from the perspective of the poor this looks like an ideologically motivated distortion, the perspective of Israelite rulers who did not want the class elements of the foundational story to remain dominant.

2. The theory that the unity of Israel was based on their social existence as pastors of animal flocks. This sociological theory about the original unity of Israel was developed in Germany by Albrecht Alt, and followed by

Martin Noth. It postulates that the opposition between Israel and Canaan, a primary datum that any theory must explain, was the natural opposition between those who wish to use the land for pasturing flocks and those who use it for planting grains and other crops. The tribes of pastoralists will have united in time because of their common life-style and to present a united front to the peasants who used the land for crops.

The patriarchal stories reveal the coexistence in Canaan of cattle tenders like Abraham with the kings of peasant populations like the king of Gerar (Genesis 20). The story about the conflict between Isaac and the inhabitants of Beersheba would be a reflection of this usually peaceful coexistence (Gen. 26:15-25). At first it would have been sufficient to establish agreements so that in the summer (the dry season) the pastoralists could use the stubble on the harvested fields for their flocks, while in the wintertime when the fields were planted they would withdraw to the semi-arid zones of the land. They would also use the hills that were without cultivation to pasture their flocks. With the passage of time and the growth of the population both peoples would have entered into conflict over the control of the choicest lands. These conflicts would be the ones described in Joshua 1–11 and through Judges.

This is an attractive theory, because it can account in social terms for the conflict between Canaanites and Israelites. It has been criticized, however, with the anthropological observation that peoples who devote themselves exclusively to tending animals are practically unknown. It is an activity usually combined with cultivation of the land. It is also difficult for this theory to account for the fact that these pastoral peoples of Canaan received the Hebrews who arrived from Egypt after their Exodus from slavery there.

3. A peasant insurrection. Recently there has been the scientific development of a theory that proposes that the unity of the tribes emerged from their common rebellion against the kings of the cities in the land of Canaan. This theory is associated with the name of the United States exegete Norman K. Gottwald.

To understand this theory it will be helpful to remember our description of the tributary mode of production. The villages, which made up the productive base of society, could very well subsist without the king and his apparatus of government, especially in a land like Palestine where no major hydraulic works were necessary for a subsistence agriculture. The peasant insurrection that is proposed as the basis for tribal unity would have been the rejection of domination by kings in the name of an egalitarian peasant society. The conditions of perennial conflict among the kings of Canaan in the fourteenth and thirteenth centuries B.C.E. will have provided the conditions that led to these peasant revolts. The kings could not guarantee the security of the villages, the main contribution expected of kings in a land where agriculture depended only on rainfall.

The possibility of successful revolt was provided by the presence of considerable unpopulated areas in the hills of Canaan. A small migration could put the population of any village in an unpopulated area that could be cleaned and submitted to cultivation. In addition, the fourteenth century saw the introduction of two technological advances that may have assisted in opening the hills to agriculture. The use of slaked lime to line cisterns in order to retain water made it possible to store sufficient water for highland agriculture, and this was the moment of the introduction of iron implements in the Ancient Near East, although their usefulness on a wide scale is not securely documented.

In the biblical texts there is one story of a migration from the plain to the hills: In Judges 17–18 it is said that the tribe of Dan left the plain around the cities of Zorah and Eshtaol to settle in the highlands of Galilee in the area of Laish. According to this theory several of the conflicts surrounding the so-called conquest of Canaan in Joshua and Judges would have been incidents taking place during various migrations of this sort.

From the point of view of the historian the big advantage of this theory is that it explains why the story of the group that came from Egypt became the founding history for the whole tribal alliance. All had been through similar experiences in their own past! It also puts Israel's faith in a God who liberates oppressed peoples on a material base in social movements of liberation. It accounts for the commandment not to have other gods alongside Yahweh as well. This was a class struggle, and any other god might legitimate the return to slavery under human kings, the class enemy of the peasant tribes.

The difficulty faced by this theory is the lack of texts that speak in unambiguous terms of insurrections in Canaan. Only the insurrection in Egypt remains in the texts. This absence must be explained as the result of the intentional work of erasing a subversive memory once Israel had ceased to be a tribal nation in order to accept its own kings (after David).

The Exodus as a Historical Event

The biblical book that bears the name of Exodus tells how, under the leadership of Moses the prophet of Yahweh, a mixed body of slaves in the service of the king of Egypt left to seek a land flowing with milk and honey. The first question we must ask the text is, Who escaped from slavery? Exodus 1:9 and other texts speak of "the children of Israel," but Exod. 1:15 and other texts speak of "the Hebrews." "Hebrew" is a variant of the same term *'apiru* found in the land of Canaan as the designation for rebel groups who did not submit to the laws of the kings. When we add to this the datum of Exod. 12:38 that "a mixed multitude went out with them," we can deduce that in the historical event those who escaped from slavery were not one big family but a sector of that social class that made up the base of Egyptian society, the peasantry. They were called "Hebrews" because they rebelled against the tasks of constructions imposed on them by the King Ramses II.

They made their exit from slavery under the leadership of Moses, the prophet of Yahweh. God took sides with those who were oppressed in their struggle for liberation. These peasant people would probably not have dared to undertake their revolutionary migration without a religion of this sort. Revolution for them became a religious act, an act of obedience to God. The struggle against the king was a struggle among the gods: on the one hand, Pharaoh, who claimed the right of life and death over all Egyptians, and on the other Yahweh, who was attentive to the cries of the oppressed. For this reason, in order to maintain revolutionary fidelity, it was necessary to keep exclusive loyalty to Yahweh among the gods. Any other god might lead them again into slavery. Yahweh liberated them.

Once they reached Palestine, the "Levites," as they began to call themselves, found a multiplicity of peasant movements installed in the hills where they had escaped from the domination of the kings of the plains and the valleys. The result of this fruitful union was the creation of the nation of tribes called Israel, a nation that confessed itself the people of Yahweh, the God who had brought their mothers and fathers up out of slavery in Egypt.

The Organization of the Nation

A defining characteristic of all the movements of insurrection and migration that shaped the nation Israel was the rejection of kings (see, for example, Judg. 8:22-23; 9:7-15), and because monarchy was the only form of state that was known at the time, this meant in effect a rejection of the state as an expression for their nation. For the Canaanites of the day this no doubt made the Israelites "servants who are breaking away from their masters" (1 Sam. 25:10). Nevertheless, Israelite life was not disordered. Its order was regulated by the people's law, which was attributed to Yahweh. It was said that Yahweh had revealed these laws to Moses on Mount Sinai.

We call these laws people's law because, lacking any State authorities, they were administered by the elders of the people. We also call them people's law in the sense that they were not preserved in writing but were transmitted by the oral tradition of the people. The case of Boaz and the inheritance of Elimelech of Bethlehem is a magnificent example (Ruth 4:1-12). Israelite people's law forbade the sale of the land of an Israelite to another person (this was later codified in Lev. 25:23-31). It also provided special measures to avoid allowing the property of a man who died without sons to pass into another family (Deut. 25:5-10). In the case of Elimelech this was the problem; he died without leaving descendents. His relative Boaz took upon himself the right and the obligation to perpetuate the family. In order to do so he had to appear before a jury of elders to prove his right and announce his intentions.

The interrelations among Israelites were understood in the same fashion as the internal organizations of the villages in all the societies of the period, by kinship. The tribes were conceived as so many enormous families, and, at least in theory, the tribes were linked together by their descent from the sons of Jacob. Although this family unity was real, it was the result of a prior revolutionary unity and was not the cause of that unity as Kaufmann proposes in his reconstruction of Israelite origins.

The defense of the tribes was done through a call for volunteer warriors in times of external threat. The clearest case of this is the popular militia called up by Deborah to fight against the Canaanites who were under the orders of King Sisera (Judges 5). The wars fought under Gideon of Manasseh (Judges 6–8) and Jephthah of Gilead (Judges 10–11) are examples of the same phenomenon. This was in contrast to the professional armies of the Canaanite kings. A military disadvantage for Israel was the lack of horses and war chariots, heavy weapons that a volunteer army cannot sustain.

Yahweh, God, was the king of the tribes of Israel (Judges 8:22-23; 1 Sam. 8:7; Num. 23:22; Deut. 33:4-5). In practical terms this meant that the peasants of Israel paid tribute to nobody. Their only "tributes" were the firstborn of their flocks and the first fruits of their harvests which they offered to Yahweh. In the most common offerings, the *zebachim* and the *selammim*, the sacrificed animal was shared among the priest, the offering-bearer, his guests, and Yahweh (God's portion was consumed by fire). This meant that the tribute was not given over for the use of another, but it was shared in a great celebration in which God also took part. The most complete description of the sacrifices practiced in biblical Israel is given in Leviticus 1–7.

We can represent the social organization of tribal Israel graphically in the following manner:

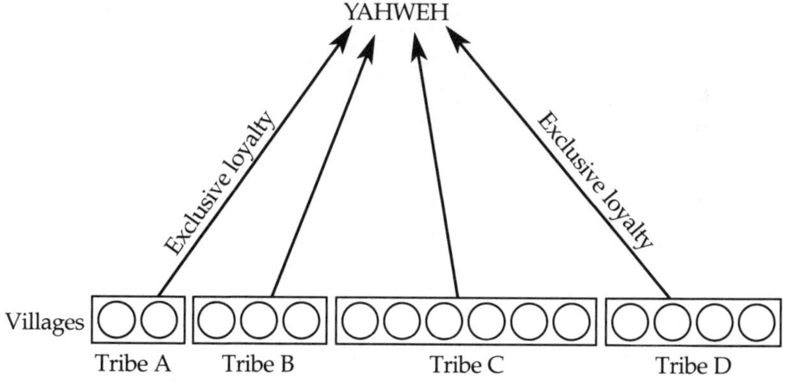

Diagram 2

The Pre-Israelite Patriarchs

When the various Israelite tribes in Canaan accepted as their own the story of the liberation from slavery (the Exodus) they did not reject their own prehistory. The traditions surrounding the patriarchs Abraham, Isaac, and Jacob preserve the memory of the leaders of the tribes in a time prior to the formation of the tribal alliance called Israel.

Very little can be derived from these stories about the prehistory of the tribes. We can deduce that Isaac belonged to the semi-arid regions of southern Palestine. In the territorial distribution of the tribes in Joshua 13–19 this area was given to the tribe of Simeon, so it is probable that these traditions belong to that tribe.

Following the same line of reasoning, Jacob belonged to the central Israelite tribes, Ephraim and Manasseh, and Abraham to the tribe of Judah. The genealogical link, which made Abraham the father of Isaac and grandfather of Jacob, was made after the Israelite alliance was secure and would serve to recognize that unity through a posited common family tree.

3

Kings Arise over the Tribes of Israel 1050–931 B.C.E.

Saul Organizes a Professional Army, the Prophetic Reaction

In the second half of the eleventh century B.C.E. lifelong leaders emerged from the midst of the tribes of Israel who took the title of *melech,* "king," a widely recognized institution in the Ancient Near East. According to the texts that describe the incident, it was a response to both internal and external pressures.

The internal problem mentioned in the texts is the corruption of the charismatic judges in the administration of justice (1 Sam. 8:5). Recent research into the agriculture practiced in the hills of Ephraim and Judah (see bibliography, David C. Hopkins, Frank S. Frick) suggests another cause that the texts do not mention. Agriculture in the highlands of Palestine was precarious. It was intensive and required the use of terraces on the mountain slopes. These terraces were difficult to construct and maintain. Another reason for agriculture's precariousness was its dependence on rainfall, which in this area was not regular enough to guarantee benefits of the peasants' labor every year. Finally, the modest quality of the soils required that they be left to rest every second year for adequate results.

All of this being the case, each village tried to diversify its production, combining perennial plants, mainly olives and grapes, with the annuals, which provided basic grains: barley and wheat. Once terraces had been built and cisterns carved in the rock, the result of long and arduous toil, it would have been possible to attain a more or less stable production. Under these conditions a certain accumulation would take place which, however, would be unequal. Accumulation would be greater in those microclimates exposed to the rains on the western slopes of the hills. Regions with better soils would also produce greater accumulation than those with poorer soils.

This social context determined the emergence of leaders with great ambitions from the families of the privileged villages. For economic reasons (the distribution of excesses), political reasons (the family cohesion around the "father"), and military reasons (the defense against villages less favorably situated), this sort of situation favored the emergence of proto-state structures. Similar processes have been observed by anthropologists in Africa.

The main reason for the emergence of kings given in the biblical texts was the external pressure exerted by the Philistines since the middle of the eleventh century. This people had come from the sea to impose itself on the cities of the plain that were situated between the hills and the sea, especially the five cities of Gath, Gaza, Ashkelon, Ekron, and Ashdod. From this political base they organized strong armies with horses and chariots, and were able to establish military posts in the mountains to gather tribute from the Israelite peasants. The volunteer organization of defense in the tribes of Israel made it difficult to face this force. This external pressure combined with the internal forces we have just examined to create a social climate receptive to political centralization.

Saul the Benjaminite was able to take advantage of the situation. Saul appeared in public when he led the volunteers of the tribes in their defense against the Ammonites (1 Samuel 11). He acted like one of the military "judges" of previous times, like Deborah and Gideon, but now there was a strong movement to make him the king over Israel. In this manner it became possible to maintain a permanent army to take charge of the defense of the nation. According to 1 Samuel 11, everything culminated in his coronation by the representatives of all the people at Gilgal.

Saul organized an army that at first numbered about three thousand men. He challenged the Philistines by killing a military governor whom they maintained in the mountains of Ephraim (1 Sam. 13:2-3). Saul incorporated into his army every strong and brave man he found, and with their help he dedicated himself to making war throughout his kingship, as it is stated in the summary of his government (1 Sam. 14:47-52).

According to the texts, Saul was made "king" by the tribes. Still, it is important to note the limits of his government. He did not have, as was customary in antiquity, either an official priesthood with its temple or a civil apparatus for collecting taxes (tribute). These "deficiencies" are reflected in the fact that he had no capital city. Apparently, he continued to live in his home town, Gibeah of Benjamin, a small city, which probably did not even have a surrounding wall. The lack of a secure capital hindered the development of a complete state apparatus. The most natural interpretation of 1 Sam. 22:7 is that Saul began to accumulate royal lands, which accords with what was said previously about the conditions for the emergence of lifelong leaders in the hills. It is likely that his army could sustain itself in large measure from the booty it acquired in its constant wars. The overall effect is a state still in an incipient stage, which we might diagram as follows:

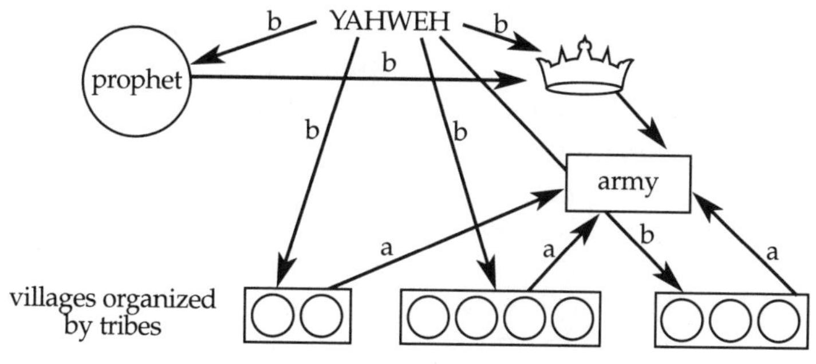

Diagram 3

The arrows marked *b* represent lines of authority. Yahweh remained the great King, before whose laws Saul had to submit and whose messenger, the prophet Samuel, had authority over Saul. The arrows marked *a* represent the tribute of the tribes, which was rendered more to the army in the form of brave young men of war than to the king himself in the form of material sustenance. It is not evident that there were social classes at this time, one subject to another. There were differences in the division of labor between those who produced (the villages) and those who were dedicated to defense (the king and the army), but apparently without any leisure class.

The tribes' reorganization to give themselves an army with professional status and quality represented a dangerous step backward in the direction of the old Egyptian slavery in the eyes of those who maintained a clear memory of the revolution directed by Yahweh and by his prophet Moses. The texts, which do not give the appearance of being contemporary but rather the result of much reflection during a period of years, make the prophet Samuel the spokesperson for those who saw this danger. It is worthwhile to study 1 Samuel 8 and 1 Samuel 12 to appreciate these warnings.

According to 1 Samuel 8, Samuel initially rejected the proposal of the elders of the tribes that he should give them a king. The prophet repeated the argument of Gideon that to appoint a king "like all the nations" would be tantamount to rejecting the kingship of Yahweh (1 Sam. 8:4, 7). Nevertheless, acting as a prophet in the name of Yahweh, he authorized the naming of a king. In doing so he warned that Israel by naming a king entered into a dangerous path that could only end in slavery (1 Sam. 8:10-17).

An aged Samuel gives his purported farewell discourse in view of his impending death in 1 Samuel 12 (although the sequence of the narrative suggests that he lived on several years). In the text, both Samuel and the people recognize that Israel committed a grave sin in asking for a king. But Samuel acknowledges that all may go well before Yahweh if both the people and their king "fear Yahweh and serve him, if you listen to his voice and do not rebel against the commands of Yahweh" (1 Sam. 12:14). This same prophet Samuel later withdrew his support for Saul, the king whom the tribes chose and whose election Samuel had blessed in the name of Yahweh in whose name he had initially granted it (1 Sam. 15:28, 34-35).

Diagram 3 represents the idea contained in these texts that Yahweh continues as the supreme king of Israel. Saul is not an absolute sovereign, as Canaanite kings were. He is subject to the laws of Yahweh that were revealed to his servant Moses on Sinai, and to the living word of Yahweh addressed to him by the prophet Samuel.

A Nation-State Displaces the Tribal Nation: David, His Government, and the New Theology

Shortly before 1000 B.C.E. David emerged as a king of Israel who besides being a military leader was also a political leader who would profoundly alter the nature of the nation. It is necessary to study him with care.

David appeared in public life as a soldier in the army of Saul. It is probable that the wonderful story of his feat in defeating the Philistine giant Goliath is a case of transferal because the same deed is attributed to Elhanan (2 Sam. 21:19). It was brave deeds in the battlefield that led to the popular refrain, "Saul has killed his thousands, but David his ten thousands" (1 Sam. 18:7). He married Michal, one of the daughters of Saul, a matter that was intimately tied to his military championship in the popular memory (1 Sam. 18:17-30).

The time came when David broke with Saul and the army of Israel to withdraw to his native Judah to organize his own army there (1 Sam. 22:1-2). He sent his parents abroad for their protection and started a guerrilla war in the hills of Judah (1 Sam. 22:3-5). The tactics David used to maintain his army with "voluntary" contributions from the citizenry are revealed in 1 Samuel 25. Nabal the shepherd was asked for a contribution in light of the fact that David's men roamed the hills and had caused no harm to his workers or his animals. David was a local patriot and up to a point such contributions might be understood as support of a worthy cause. But the story also shows the limits of this strategy. Nabal took the request as the work of thugs asking for "protection money" and rejected it.

David's strategy was good, but if the struggle prolonged itself the strategy would boomerang. He would be seen as a burden and a nuisance to the population and his cause would lose its political base of support in resentment against northern leadership and the desire for local control. For these reasons David withdrew with his men to Philistine territory and there became a "servant" of King Achish of Gath, from whom he received the town of Ziklag as his feudal domain (1 Sam. 27:1-12).

On the occasion of Saul's death in combat with the Philistines, Saul's son Ishbaal (or Ishboshet) became the king of Israel, although he had to withdraw to Transjordan and govern from the city of Mahanaim (2 Sam. 2:8-10). David took advantage of the deaths of Saul and his son Jonathan (killed in the same battle at Mount Gilboa) and the weak position of Ishbaal to return openly to Judah, where he was crowned king of Judah by the elders of the people (2 Sam. 2:1-4). For a brief time, then, Israel had two kings.

Ishbaal was assassinated by his own men after only seven years on the throne (2 Sam. 4:1-12) and David was declared king by a delegation of elders from the tribes who went to visit him at Hebron in Judah where he had established his capital (2 Sam. 5:1-5). David was an astute politician who knew how to take advantage of this situation. His first act was to conquer a new capital city, a matter that requires our attention.

Jerusalem was an ancient city, which already appears in the letters of Tel-el-amarna in the fourteenth century. Its inhabitants were Jebusites. When the tribes of Israel had settled in the hills, the Jebusites of Jerusalem refused to join them (in contrast to the Gibeonites and the Shechemites) and the Israelites were not able to subdue them (as they did with the dwellers of Hazor). At this time, then, Jerusalem was a monarchical enclave in the middle of the mountains controlled by the tribes of peasant Israelites. Its existence was an obstacle for the communication between Judah to the south and Benjamin and the other tribes to the north. This enforced separation helps to understand the separatist tendencies of Judah in Israel's history. Immediately after being designated king of all Israel, about 1000 B.C.E., David conquered the city with his own army and named it the "City of David" (2 Sam. 5:6-12). It was a step of enormous consequence for the future of Israel.

Some reasons for the importance of the conquest of Jerusalem are the following: (1) its geographical location between the two major historical divisions of Israel, Judah, and the northern tribes; (2) its strategic military location, because it was situated on a hill with easy access only from the north, and it was surrounded by walls; (3) David conquered the city with his own army, making it the City of David, meaning that it was not a part of any of the tribes with no elders to consult in this city so that David was absolute lord; (4) the citizens of Jerusalem had a long experience with monarchic government, including a quarry of government officials for the new king of Israel, a nation with no experience with public administration; hence the importance of the fact that David did not kill its inhabitants in spite of what Yahweh demanded be done to the inhabitants of Canaanite cities according to some Israelite traditions (Deut. 20:16-18).

We have an incomplete sketch of the administrative cupola that David established over his reign (2 Sam. 8:15-18). It shows a curious duality both in the army (with two generals, Joab and Benaiah) and in the religious establishment (with two high priests, Abiathar and Zadok). One possible explanation is that Joab and Abiathar represented the traditional forces of Israel, while Benaiah (who headed the military elite of the Cherethites and the Pelethites) and Zadok represented the new monarchic force, with no commitments to the tribes. Zadok may have been a Jebusite priest taken by David to share the religious direction of his kingdom with Abiathar, a survivor of the priestly family of Shiloh and Nob in the territory of Ephraim.

It is also convenient to reflect on the many wars of conquest undertaken by David as king of Israel (2 Sam. 8:1-14). David carved out an empire for himself and for Israel. Why? A strong suspicion is that in this manner David could maintain a significant state bureaucracy without imposing tribute on the tribes of Israel. These tribes had a history of resisting any tribute, and to impose tributes would have been politically explosive. Having the Edomites, the Moabites, the Philistines, the Ammonites, and the Aramaeans under his control, David could maintain his palaces, his army, and his capital city with the tribute collected among these peoples while allowing the tribes of Israel freedom from the heavy tribute that would otherwise have been necessary to support kingship.

Even so, David had to face several movements of rebellion that emerged in the midst of the tribes. The most important uprising was that headed by his son Absalom who succeeded in being crowned king in Hebron, the old Judahite capital of David (2 Sam. 15:7-12), and was eventually able to take control of Jerusalem itself for a time (2 Sam. 15–17). Another important uprising was headed by Sheba of Benjamin. His movement took up a slogan that was to have importance later in Israel, "We have no part in David, nor any portion in the son of Jesse. Each one to his tents, oh Israel!" (2 Sam. 20:1). Benjamin was the tribe from which Saul had come, and there were those who suspected that David was not innocent in the deaths of Saul and his sons. But, in spite of the dissent that David had to face, he is remembered in the Bible as a good king. This is no doubt due to his military successes and the care he took to consider the prerogatives the tribes of Israel claimed for themselves.

David introduced some novelties that changed the nature of the religion of Yahweh. The first matter was to bring to his new capital the ark of the covenant, where the tables of law were kept which God had given to Moses. He established a new feast day to celebrate this transfer (2 Samuel 6, Psalm 132). He also bought a piece of property in order to place the tent for the ark on crown property (2 Samuel 24). This, plus naming chief priests as government employees, shows that David was following the way of the kings of the nations in establishing a controlled system of worship under direct obedience to the king. In tributary societies such as that of Canaan this was decisive, because it was necessary to justify before the people the total domination that kings exercised over them. Kings needed to be recognized as gods or the sons of a god so that their absolute control of the lands, the animals, and the bodies of their people would have a seal of legitimacy.

It was perfectly natural that David should wish to build a temple for Yahweh, the God of Israel (2 Samuel 7). It was natural from the point of view of the king, but the prophet Nathan opposed the project. His opposition probably came from his recognition of the danger of allowing the king to control the worship of Yahweh, the liberator of the poor. In the name of Yahweh, Nathan said:

> I have not lived in a house since the day I brought up the people of Israel from Egypt to this day, but I have been moving about in a tent and a tabernacle. Wherever I have moved about among all the people of Israel, did I ever speak a word with any of the tribal leaders of Israel, whom I commanded to shepherd my people Israel, saying, "Why have you not built me a house of cedar?" (2 Sam. 7:6-7).

David did not feel that he could oppose the direct prohibition of the prophet of Yahweh and he abstained from his intention of building a temple.

This royal abstention lasted only a generation, however, for Solomon, David's successor on the throne of Israel, built the temple for Yahweh on the land that his father had acquired for the tent in the city of Jerusalem. It was probably in Solomon's time that the tradition of the words of Nathan was altered by adding the words that make the prohibition apply only to David and not to his successor on the throne (verse 13, which reads like an interpolation in the oracle of Nathan in 2 Sam. 7:5-16).

We can represent the Israelite society as organized by David in the following manner showing the emergence of the state:

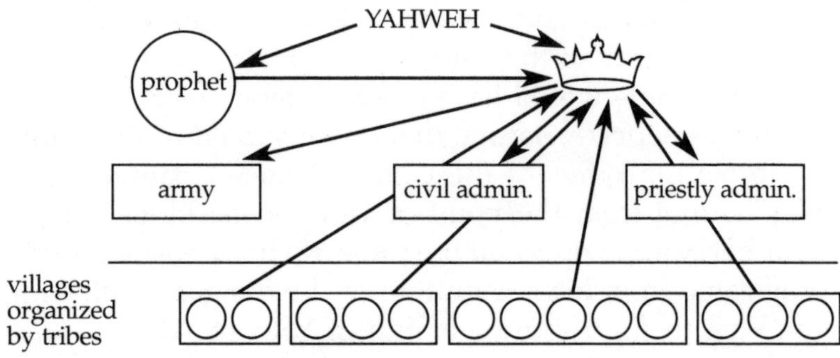

Diagram 4

In many ways the Davidic state was similar to the Canaanite states that the tribes had rejected. It had an army, a priesthood, and a civilian bureaucracy, which were directly dependent on the will and the financial support of the king, as did the Canaanites. These bureaucracies did not represent the tribes. The tribes were now related directly to the king, and only through him to the state bureaucracies.

Even so, there were some limits on tyranny. The first was without a doubt people's organization. The villages did not each face the king alone, as was the case in Egypt and in Canaan. The villages were organized in tribes and this union made it possible to face the king with greater strength than would otherwise have been possible.

Another limit on tyranny was the general recognition of the supreme authority of Yahweh. This authority was discharged through the laws of Sinai, which were also binding on the king (as in the case of Bathsheba whose husband he had eliminated in order to take her, 2 Samuel 11–12), and through the prophet of Yahweh, Nathan, in the days of David. This second limit was no more than purely spiritual, because Nathan had no armies at his disposal. Nevertheless, popular support made it a political force to take into account.

David had succeeded in reestablishing a class society within the nation Israel, a nation born out of revolution. David's government was not oppressive because he was able to live largely from the tribute of subject peoples, and because he showed respect for tribal traditions. Nevertheless, he set in place the pieces for the open oppression, which his son Solomon imposed after his death.

From the theological perspective, the rise of a "royal ideology" or "Davidic theology" was most important. It was produced by the royal priesthood at the court. It is likely that not all of this theology was elaborated under the reign of David, but it was he who initiated it and to this day the psalms, the highest expression of this theology, are mostly attributed to David. For a reading from the perspective of the poor the Davidic theology is ambiguous because it can be used, as in fact it has been used, as the support and legitimation of the oppression of the poor. This does not mean that the Davidic theology ought to be rejected outright; it contains and elaborates authentic elements of the faith of Yahweh the God of the Exodus, and for this reason it became an important source for the messianism of Jesus. It may be said that since the days of David the theology of Israel had two foci, the Exodus as the liberation of the people of God, and the election of David as the son of Yahweh and defender of the people of God.

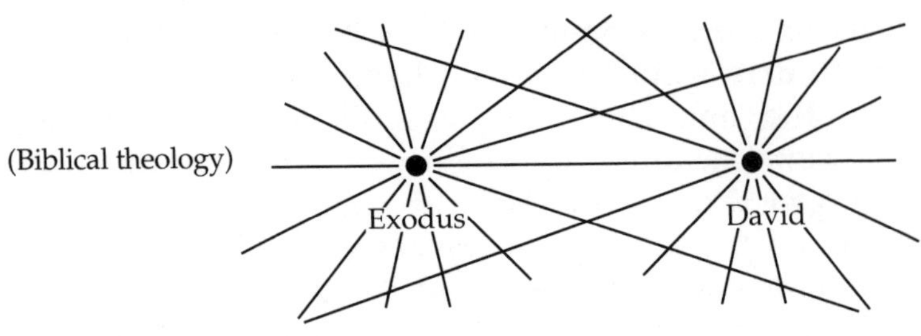

Diagram 5

Davidic theology was drawn up by the priests of the king in the city of Jerusalem. Psalms is the book of prayer and celebration of the Jerusalem Temple. This explains the importance that the themes of Davidic theology play in the Psalms. Some of the themes included are listed here:

The establishment of an eternal covenant between Yahweh and David is the very heart of this theology. It can be seen in its fullness in Psalm 89. In Exodus theology the covenant was established at Sinai between Yahweh and the people of Israel, through the mediation of Moses. This alliance promised that Yahweh would be the God of the people as long as the people kept his commandments (Exod. 19:3-8). On the other hand, Davidic theology, which is found in this and other psalms, indicates an alliance or covenant that is established between Yahweh and David (Ps. 89:4-5). Besides, this covenant is eternal and unbreakable because it rests on an oath of Yahweh (Ps. 89:35-36). Should the king violate the commandments of Yahweh he will be punished, but Yahweh will never withdraw the covenant (Ps. 89:31-34).

An important piece in the legitimation of this covenant was an oracle attributed to Nathan, the prophet of Yahweh, which, in its significant core states, "Yahweh declares to you that Yahweh will make you a house. When your days are fulfilled and you lie down with your ancestors, I will raise up your offspring after you, who shall come forth from your body, and I will establish his kingdom. . . . Your house and your kingdom shall be made sure forever before me; your throne shall be established forever" (2 Sam. 7:12-16). The effect of this astounding oracle was not only to throw Yahweh's authority behind David but also behind the Davidic dynasty forever. Any alternative line of kingship that might emerge from any of the tribes was declared illegitimate and contrary to the will of Yahweh from the outset!

An expression of the election of David is that Yahweh declares that the kings in Jerusalem are God's own sons (by a sort of adoption). Psalm 2 is a liturgy of enthronement for new kings. Its central words are a decree of Yahweh: "You are my son; I have today begotten you. Ask me and I will give you the nations for an inheritance" (Ps. 2:7-8). It seems surprising to us who are quite removed from the ideologies of kingship that this element of the royal ideology of the surrounding nations should have entered into the royal theology at Jerusalem.

A corollary of the election of the king was the election of the city of Jerusalem by Yahweh to be his "resting place" (Ps. 132:13-14). This is attributed in Psalm 132 to the diligence with which David sought a place for the ark of Yahweh.

Davidic theology did not forget that Yahweh is a God of the poor. The king whom Yahweh chooses for Zion is to become a benefactor and defender of the poor. For this reason Yahweh has made him king in his city. Psalm 72 develops this essential aspect of Davidic theology. In ancient times and in modern ones this element has made it possible to use the Psalms against tyrants like General Somoza who have oppressed and exploited the poor. The *Psalms* of poet Ernesto Cardenal show the people's potential, which is there in the Psalms in spite of their royal origin.

In the Christian church the Psalms have been read as announcements of the coming of the Messiah whom Christians affirm came in the work of Jesus. This reading gives the Psalms a new twist, which needs to be developed. Nevertheless, we must not allow the messianic reading of the Psalms to erase their original significance as the ideology that underwrote David and his descendents on a throne over Israel in a Canaanite city.

Solomon: A Temple of Yahweh Legitimates the Oppression of the People

Any account of the reign of Solomon must begin with the struggle he won over his older brother Adonijah in order to sit on the throne. Adonijah, with the help of Joab, the chief of the army, and of Abiathar, one of the chief priests, had himself proclaimed as king (1 Kings 1:1-10). This particular group of people suggests that what we have is an effort by the traditional party, the representatives of the tribes, to secure the succession to the throne. In Adonijah they seemed to have a candidate with excellent credentials. He was the fourth male born to David of a legitimate wife, Haggith, in the early days when David ruled in Hebron (2 Sam. 3:2-5). David's firstborn son, Amnon, was dead, as was the second-born, Absalom, the one who briefly tore the throne out of the hands of his father. We know nothing of the fate of the third-born, Chileab, who was also presumably dead by the end of David's reign. A public place in Jerusalem, the stone of Zoheleth beside the spring of En-Rogel was chosen as an appropriate place where the populace could join in the coronation.

The response of the party identified with the project of a full-scale monarchy responded with a palace intrigue designed to gain support for their candidate, Solomon, from an elderly David who was no longer in control of all his senses (1 Kings 1:11-40). Solomon was also a son of David, born to Bathsheba, the former wife of Uriah the Hittite. He had been born in Jerusalem within the palace.

Among the party who supported Solomon was the prophet Nathan, whose promise concerning Yahweh's choice of David was the cornerstone of the Davidic theology (2 Sam. 7:8-16). Benaiah, the general of the Cherethites and the Pelethites, and Zadoq, the high priest whose origin we suggested was Jebusite, also supported Solomon.

Once David had died, Solomon moved to consolidate his throne. He succeeded in having both Adonijah and Joab killed. He exiled Abiathar to the city of Anathoth in the tribe of Benjamin. There it seems that his family maintained itself as a priestly opposition for a long time, and from among them Jeremiah rose up over three hundred years later.

This purge of the court personnel allowed Solomon to move toward a system of government that was more efficient than the one David had built. David had felt bound to respect tribal prerogatives. Solomon did not feel tied in this respect. A list of governors administered a system of twelve districts into which Solomon divided his kingdom (1 Kings 4:7-19). Some of these districts coincided with the ancient tribal territories, but others were made out of the lands conquered by David or out of the combination of more than one tribal territory. The naming of governors over territories that had traditionally belonged to the tribes was a significant innovation. With this measure the king set aside the authorities of the people and imposed his own authorities. The administration of the nation became pyramidal.

Each of the governors was responsible for raising the tribute necessary to sustain the state apparatus during one month out of the year, with food for the numerous families of the king, for the "servants of the king," and for the war horses (1 Kings 5:1-8, or in the New Revised Standard Version Bible, 4:21-28).

Besides the tribute in kind, which was extracted from the peasant villages by the governors of the twelve districts, Solomon also introduced tribute in the form of forced labor. The manner of its introduction is significant. Basing himself on the oracle through which Nathan had forbidden the building of the Temple for Yahweh, now emended to authorize the son of David to do what David himself was forbidden to realize, Solomon undertook to build a luxurious Temple for Yahweh. To accomplish the task he organized the population into work brigades, thirty thousand to bring fine wood from Lebanon, sixty thousand burden bearers, and eighty thousand stonecutters (1 Kings 5:15-32 [5:1-18]). Each work brigade spent one month at the work site and returned for two months to cover the field tasks at home. He put three thousand overseers above these workers from among the servants of the king. The general administrator of all this forced labor was a certain Adoram or Adoniram, son of Abda (1 Kings 4:6).

When this monumental task was finished, Solomon took advantage of the organized labor to build better defenses for Jerusalem, palaces for his many wives, garrison and storage cities like Gezer, Beth Horon the Lower, Baalath, and Tamar, and to build stables for his war horses and chariots (1 Kings 9:15-24). (The statement in 1 Kings 9:22 that he did not use Israelites in the brigades of forced labor contradicts the evidence of chapter 5 and also 1 Kings 11:28; it must be taken as an attempt to conceal the facts of Solomon's oppressive government.)

In addition to the wealth Solomon derived from the exploitation of the population of Israel, he cultivated a lucrative international trade. He acquired a fleet of ships to navigate the Red Sea (1 Kings 9:26-28). He became an arms merchant, buying Cilician horses in order to sell them to Egypt, and Egyptian war chariots to sell them to Aram (1 Kings 10:26-29). He also provided himself with abundant weapons of war for his own chariotry.

The Yahweh Temple in Jerusalem functioned on royal property as a royal institution; its priests were state bureaucrats with an important role to play in the social structure. With their theology and feasts they assured that Solomon enjoyed social legitimacy. They made it known that Yahweh, the same God who had brought Israel out of slavery in Egypt now blessed Solomon, his chosen king. In order to read with critical discernment the praises accorded to Solomon in the Bible it is necessary to resort to the theological key that guides any reading from the perspective of the poor, the Exodus. With this key in mind, it is obvious that the Yahweh of Solomon is not the same God who heard the cries exacted from the slaves in Egypt by their oppressors. The God of the poor had been captured by the dominators in order to legitimate the oppression of the peasants of Israel.

The social structure of the kingdom of Solomon is much like the classic model of the tributary mode of production, with the sole difference that the king was still formally subject to the law of Yahweh. Nevertheless, we do not hear of any prophet who placed Solomon under the limits of the Word of Yahweh.

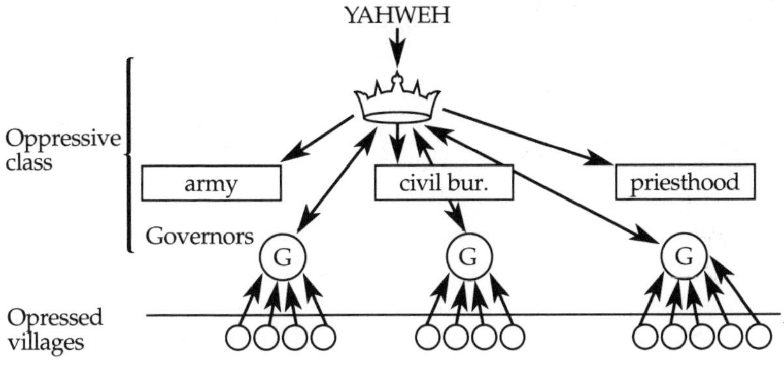

Diagram 6

In this social scheme popular organization (the tribes) is replaced by the districts, which reflect the royal administration and have no base in people's organizations. The arrows that point upward from the villages represent the tribute extracted from them for the benefit of the king through the mediation of the district governors. This tribute includes both a part of the production of the fields and a part of the peasants' labor. The arrows that come down from above represent the authority of the king to dispose of his servants, naming or displacing these bureaucrats who serve at the royal pleasure.

Samuel had said it well, "You shall be his slaves!" (1 Sam. 8:17).

The Literary Production of This Period

The earliest major Israelite documents we can discern in the Bible come from this early monarchical period. Older pieces in the Bible are single poems set within larger and later works (the oracles of Balaam, the Song of Deborah, and so on). This Solomonic period saw a flourishing of literature under the influence of the court. Solomon was remembered in later days as a wise man, probably because of the intellectual climate at the court in his days. Major narrative works from this setting have been preserved after being included in later literary works. There is a broad agreement among scholars that the "Yahwist," or J (so named because of the term that writer uses for God), of the Pentateuch and the "history of the succession" in 2 Samuel are from this period and this court setting.

For over a hundred years modern interpreters of the Pentateuch have shared a broad agreement that this major and complex narrative is the result of the combination of three versions of the history of the national origins of Israel, with the addition of a speech attributed to Moses, in Deuteronomy. Since the important work of Julius Wellhausen last century it has also been widely recognized that of the three narrative sources in the Pentateuch the "Yahwist" is the oldest. It is also the narrative with the greatest literary grace and compositional quality.

The content of the J narrative, like that of classic Greek theater, is given by the people's oral tradition. This tradition took shape during the tribal period prior to the monarchy. It is organized around four (or five) themes: (1) The promise of land and abundant descendents to the patriarchs, (2) the Exodus from slavery in Egypt, (3) the granting of the law of Yahweh on Mount Sinai, and (4) the wilderness wandering, with its double emphasis on the grace of Yahweh which sustained the people, and the rebellions of Israel. A fifth theme of popular tradition, the fulfillment of the promise of land, is little developed by the J writer, who deals only with the victories over Sihon and Og of Transjordan.

Since the brilliant work of the major twentieth-century exegete Gerhard von Rad, it has been widely recognized that the creation and the primal history (the flood, the tower of Babel, and so on) were not part of the traditional history of Israel. These stories were taken from the general culture of the Ancient Near East. For his service at court Solomon drew intellectuals from various countries who were familiar with the shared elements of culture among them. From this lore, the wise men of the court of Solomon took the stories of creation, the flood, the tower of Babel and others, adapted them to Israelite theology, and placed them as an introduction to Israel's history, thus giving it a universal setting.

The point of view from which the history is told is Judahite, that is, southern. In the blessing of Jacob (Genesis 49) and the oracles of Balaam (Numbers 24) there are unmistakable allusions that point to the kingdom of David and Solomon, which would have been viewed by the J writer as the culmination of Israel's history.

The other great literary production of this period was given its classical interpretation by Leonhard Rost in 1926. It is preserved in 2 Samuel 9–20, continued in 1 Kings 1–2. It appears to be the tale by an eyewitness of the events inside the court of David, culminating in the surprising succession to his throne by Solomon, a son who was not the elder and whose mother's marital legitimacy was clouded by murder and adultery. The fine narrative style and the sophisticated theology of this work have long caused the admiration of biblical interpreters. For its time it shows a remarkable historical consciousness, so much that it can justly be called the earliest historical writing of humankind. In contrast to popular theology of all times, the role of God is handled discretely. History is not interrupted with divine manifestations, although God is certainly at work through various human agents. It is clear evidence of the enlightened ambience of the Solomonic court. Even so, it appears to have been written as a sophisticated piece of political apology, a defense of the fact that Solomon was David's successor on the throne at Jerusalem. Its author was a high-level political writer who obviously had a much larger audience in mind than those who commissioned his work!

4
The Tribes Rebel against the Davidic Dynasty 931-884 B.C.E.

During Solomon's reign there was a rebellion of the tribes of Israel led by Jeroboam of Ephraim. Jeroboam was a high functionary responsible for the forced labor crews of the "house of Joseph," which probably means the districts of Ephraim and Benjamin (1 Kings 11:26-28). When the revolt was defeated Jeroboam fled to Egypt where the king, Shishak, gave him asylum (1 Kings 11:40).

Taking advantage of Solomon's death in the year 931 B.C.E. and of the discontent that prevailed in the tribes, Jeroboam returned and organized an assembly of Israel in Shechem, an ancient and important city of Ephraim. The tribal elders summoned the young Rehoboam, son of Solomon, to appear before them "to proclaim him king" (1 Kings 12:1). Nevertheless, before consenting to proclaim the king they put to the young man a list of demands, "lighten the hard service of your father and his heavy yoke that he placed on us and we will serve you" (1 Kings 12:4).

Two versions of the assembly at Shechem in 931 have come down to us, one in the Masoretic Text (MT), the ancient Hebrew Bible, and the other in the Septuagint (LXX), the ancient Greek Bible. The latter was the one known to the earliest Christians and used by them for over three centuries, but modern English Bibles are translated from the former. The reconstruction of the events surrounding the Israelite uprising must take both texts into consideration. The Spanish scholar Julio C. Trebolle Barrera has shown the relative priority of the LXX at this particular point.

It appears that after Jeroboam and his followers had placed their demands before Rehoboam, the young king sent to consult the elders of the tribes, the very leaders whom his father had displaced with his governors. These endorsed the demands of Jeroboam (1 Kings 12:24). In consultation later with his own counselors "who ate at the table with him" it was decided to maintain a hard line in the belief that otherwise the popular demands would have no end (1 Kings 12:24rLXX). Whether this sequence of events represents what actually happened or not, it surely represents truthfully the social dynamics at work in the situation. The MT reduces the discussion to an internal debate at the court between the older counselors and the younger ones, a much less useful narrative for clarifying the social dynamics (1 Kings 12:6-15).

Faced with the flat rejection of their demands by Rehoboam, the people refused to make him king and withdrew from the negotiations chanting the old slogan of Sheba the Benjaminite, "What part have we with David? We have no inheritance in the son of Jesse! To your tents, oh Israel! Look now to your own house, David!" (1 Kings 12:16). They completed their rejection of David's house and what it stood for by stoning to death Adoram, the supreme chief of the task forces of the kingdom (1 Kings 12:18). Rehoboam was able to escape to Jerusalem, where he was able to draw to himself the tribe of Judah and, as it seems, the larger part of Benjamin (1 Kings 12:21).

The tribes of Israel then proclaimed Jeroboam as king and he made Shechem his provisional capital (1 Kings 12:20, 25). Nevertheless, Shechem was not his city in the same sense that Jerusalem was David's city. Shechem was an old city, long incorporated into the tribal nation Israel. Memory of the great assembly that Joshua had supposedly convoked at Shechem in the heroic days of the original revolution (Joshua 24) was alive. Jeroboam later moved his capital to Tirzah, a city within the jurisdiction of the elders of Manasseh.

The lack of a royal capital city reflects the nature of this kingdom, which arose out of a protest against the oppression of the Davidides in Jerusalem. Jeroboam was returning to a type of military leadership of the sort exercised earlier by Saul. He was responsible for the army of Israel but he did not have an elaborate system of tribute with its necessary civil bureaucracy. He did not administer a temple with its priestly personnel dependent on the crown.

Let us return for a moment to a significant factor, the prophetic support for Jeroboam's revolt. Here MT and LXX, the two ancient Bibles, differ in important facts, but both recognize the support of the prophet of Yahweh for the rebellion. According to MT it was the prophet Ahijah of Shiloh who incited Jeroboam to the first revolt, the one that failed (1 Kings 11:26-40). It does not make the oppression of Solomon the motive for the rebellion, but attributes it to Yahweh's anger with Solomon's tolerance for foreign gods, the gods of his foreign wives (1 Kings 11:33). This is not a motive completely alien to oppression, as we have seen, Yahweh was a God who could not tolerate oppression while this was not a problem for the other gods. Still, LXX is probably nearer to the truth when it affirms that it was the prophet Shemaiah of Elam who incited Jeroboam, not for the first rebellion but for the convocation of the assembly at Shechem after the death of Solomon (1 Kings 12:24oLXX).

In either case it is significant that the prophets of Yahweh responded to the cry of the tribes of Israel because of the apostasy and the oppression imposed on them. The uprising of the tribes of Israel against the house of David was able to count on the support of Yahweh and Yahweh's prophets.

It is basic for the proper and critical understanding of the books of the Kings to carefully examine the text concerning the religious measures that were taken at this juncture (1 Kings 12:26-33), and to do so with the theological key of the Exodus. Kings were written from the point of view of Jerusalem, and we have already seen how the

Temple of Jerusalem was the result of a policy of taking from the people its holy objects, such as the ark, and putting them under the control and at the service of the oppressors of the people. This causes suspicions concerning the text.

It is said that Jeroboam established places of worship at Bethel and at Dan. If we turn to the traditions of the tribes we see clearly that both Bethel and Dan were ancient centers of the worship of Yahweh. At Bethel Yahweh had appeared to the patriarch Jacob (Gen. 28:10-22), and Dan is where the tribe by that name established its religious center after their migration from Zorah and Eshtaol (Judg. 18:28-31).

The liturgical refrain, "This is your god (or 'gods,' because the Hebrew *'elohim* can be rendered as a singular or a plural), oh Israel, that brought you up out of the land of Egypt" (1 Kings 12:28), is an allusion to the traditions of the Exodus. There is nothing, from the point of view of the Exodus and the people, that is theologically dubious about either the liturgical refrain or about the places of worship that Jeroboam restored (he obviously did not found them).

The bulls at Bethel and Dan may have been understood as images of Yahweh or, more likely, as beasts on which Yahweh mounted. In Exodus 32 it is taken as a serious sin that Aaron made images of Yahweh to lead the people in the desert, thus causing the people to sin. It is taken as a violation of the commandment "You shall not make for yourself an image" (Exod. 20:4). The bulls were, therefore, questionable. But within the Temple of Jerusalem there were also images, such as the cherubim, which extended their wings to protect the ark of the covenant (1 Kings 8:6-7), and bulls in the Temple courtyard to support the sea of bronze (1 Kings 7:25). The cherubim on the ark were understood to be the seat on which Yahweh mounted (1 Sam. 4:4; Ps. 80:1). The editorial condemnation of the sanctuaries of Bethel and Dan looks suspicious. If Jeroboam was violating the Sinaitic command with his images, why are David and Solomon not condemned for the same reason? It is probable that neither David nor Jeroboam had any awareness of violating a commandment.

In summary, the worship of Yahweh, which Jeroboam sponsored, does not appear to have violated the people's traditions. On the contrary we should understand it as an attempt to return to the people their traditions, which in Jerusalem had been usurped by the kings. The frequent condemnations in Kings of those who "did evil in the sight of Yahweh, following in the way of Jeroboam the son of Nebat with which he made Israel sin" (1 Kings 15:34; 16:26; 2 Kings 13:2, and so on) are thus a Jerusalemite judgment that does not reflect the faith of the people in Yahweh, the God of the Exodus.

The religious policy of Jeroboam should not be understood as an imitation of that of David and his descendents. Neither Bethel nor Dan were royal cities. Their sanctuaries were not on crown lands. Of course the kings of Israel had an important influence on these sanctuaries, but they did not have the total control exercised on the Temple of Jerusalem. It appears that under Jeroboam the people regained some control over their faith in Yahweh.

Two elements in the social structure of Israel served as limits on the kings. The more important of these was the army, which was apparently drawn from the tribes. Its battalions were most likely organized by tribes and kept some contacts with the tribes from which they were drawn. It was from the midst of the army that new kings rose in Israel to cut off the possibility for unpopular kings to perpetuate their rule through their sons. In this manner Baasha of Issacar killed Nadab in the army camp, who was the son of Jeroboam, and took the throne in 909 (1 Kings 15:27). In 885 B.C.E. Zimri, chief of half of the chariotry, killed Elah, the son of Baasha (1 Kings 16:9). It was a violent but effective way of controlling the ambitions of the kings.

The other element of limitation on the kings was the participation of the prophets of Yahweh in public life. Ahijah of Shiloh condemned Jeroboam in the name of Yahweh, thus paving the way for a military coup against his son by Baasha (1 Kings 14:1-18 MT; the LXX version is briefer and placed earlier but is in its substance the same, 1 Kings 12:24g-nLXX). The prophet Jehu, son of Hanani, did the same thing against Baasha some years later (1 Kings 16:1-4), preparing the coup of Zimri against Baasha's son Elah. In this way Israel (in contradistinction from Judah) kept alive the tradition of the public role of the prophet of Yahweh, the role that was initiated by Samuel according to our sources. In Judah the oracle attributed to Nathan cut out the basis of further prophetic participation in politics by giving a blank check to all of the descendants of David on the Jerusalem throne.

As we can see, Israelite society had returned to a social structure similar to what had existed under Saul, which we may represent thus:

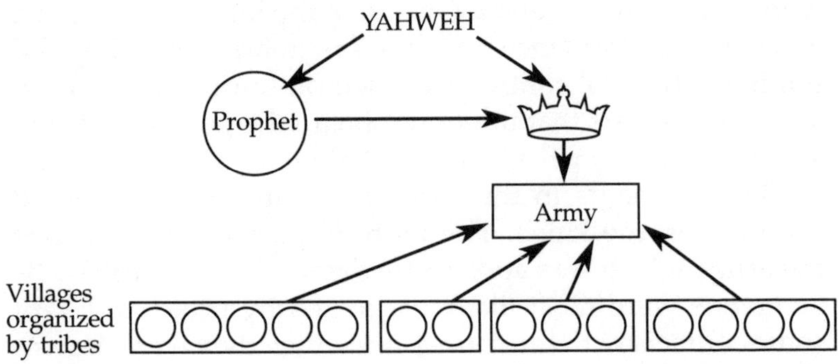

Diagram 7

The king, lacking a civilian bureaucracy and keeping an uncertain authority over the religious sanctuaries, was more than anything else a military chief, responsible to watch over the defense of the tribes. The tribes represented people's interests. Their tribute was primarily to supply the army with men and materials. There was no organized oppression of one class over another. The king had a precarious religious legitimacy that rested on the consent of

Yahweh's recognized prophet. It is easy to understand that the tribes paid for the popular control over state structures with a certain amount of instability, but the kings of Israel did not impose the tribute of work brigades to undertake the construction of palaces, temples, or even public works.

The Northern (Elohist) Version of the Traditions of the Origins

We have noted that with the emergence of a royal court that included intellectuals, the history of the origins of the nation was written down on the basis of the prior oral traditions of the tribes. Although the Yahwist writing in the Pentateuch shows a great respect for the popular traditions, it shows its southern bias. It was natural, then, that when the tribes of Israel separated from Judah, its intellectuals felt the need to produce their own written version of the traditions about national origins.

In modern biblical studies this northern history is known as the Elohist (E) version because it shows a clear preference for using the word God *'elohim* for the national God Yahweh. This preference was important in the work of isolating this writing within the Pentateuch, in which it is woven together with the Yahwist and the Priestly (P) versions of these same popular traditions.

The Elohist story of the origins of Israel is distinguished by the prominence it gives to the prophets. Abraham is presented as a prophet, as is Moses. This emphasis coincides with the role the prophets played in the religion of the tribes of the north. The Word of God is given through the prophets and the only appropriate response on the part of humans is to obey. The mediation of the prophets in the Elohist history has the effect of removing God from a direct presence in earthly affairs, if one compares it with the Yahwist. Although the Elohist is not preserved in complete form in the Pentateuch (it is the most fragmentary of the three), it is apparent that it limits itself to the four nuclei of popular tradition: patriarchs, Exodus, Sinai, and wilderness wanderings. The northern writers did not take the liberty of the Jerusalem writers in prefacing the work with the traditions of "the nations" about creation and prehistoric times.

Nothing in the Elohist history as it has been preserved in the Pentateuch allows us to date its writing. We must be satisfied to know that it was compiled in the north, perhaps at Bethel, during the period of north Israelite kingship (931–722 B.C.E.), probably early rather than late in this period.

Chronological Framework for the History of Israel

ca. 1220 B.C.E. Exodus from Egypt (Merneptah, 1224–1204)

ca. 1000 David conquers Jerusalem

931 Jeroboam and the tribes revolt against Rehoboam

884–841 Dynasty of Omri (Omri, Ahab, Ahaziah, Joram)

841–752 Dynasty of Jehu (Jehu, Joash, Jeroboam II, Zechariah)

722 Assyria destroys Samaria

640–609 Reign of Josiah (Reform)

597 Deportation of Jehoiachin to Babylon

586 Destruction of Jerusalem

538 Return under Sheshbazzar

520–515 Reconstruction of the Jerusalem Temple

445–? Nehemiah is governor

332 Alexander conquers Palestine

301–198 Ptolemaean hegemony over Palestine

167–164 Maccabean insurrection

63 Pompey conquers Jerusalem

66–70 C.E. First War with Rome, destruction of the Temple

132–35 Second War with Rome, defeat of Simon bar Cosiba

5
Omri Consolidates Power in the North 884-841 B.C.E.

In the history of Israel the dynasty of Omri (884–841) is a bleak period, a time when the kings themselves tried for reasons of state to separate the people from their exclusive loyalty to Yahweh their God. During these years two great prophets, Elijah and Elisha, rose up to lead the people in facing the crisis. But it was finally the army, as on other occasions, that put an end to this experience, which was a sad one for the people.

Omri had been a commander of the army when Zimri killed Elah the king (1 Kings 16:16). Immediately, the troops thrust him forward to be king. Zimri committed suicide, but half of the people followed a certain Tibni while the other half followed Omri. This situation lasted some time, but eventually the Omri fraction prevailed.

At this time Israel had serious problems of national defense. Judah had joined with the Aramaeans of Damascus against Israel and, as a result Israel had lost control of great extensions of its national territory. On the south Judah had taken all of Benjamin and even portions of Ephraim. Galilee had fallen in its greater part under Aramaean control as had all of Gilead (Transjordan). It was then a national priority to restore the lost territories.

Omri faced the crisis with a combination of an internal policy that sought to strengthen the state and a foreign policy based on a system of alliances.

The basis of his internal policy was to purchase a large piece of land in order to build a capital city on it, which would be the property of the crown. This new city was

Samaria (1 Kings 16:24). We ought not to doubt that he populated his new capital with persons who owed him direct personal loyalty, essentially the new government bureaucracy. He had a temple built in his new city, which he dedicated to the god Baal (1 Kings 16:32). This seems surprising, but it can be understood by the "need" to have a priesthood that would exalt the figure of the king to make him stronger politically and by the impossibility of domesticating Yahweh in such a way in Israel, the nation that had rejected similar pretensions on the part of the family of David.

Omri's foreign policy rested on the recognition that the principal enemy of Israel was Aram-Damascus. To strengthen himself he established an alliance with Tyre and Sidon, commercial cities with much wealth. He cemented this alliance by marrying his son Ahab to a Sidonian princess named Jezabel. Jezabel apparently brought with her priests of Baal so that the "diplomatic" marriage also served as a support for the interior policy by means of which Ahab was strengthening the state.

The other alliance through which he completed the design was with Judah, thus ending a half century of border wars. A daughter of Ahab, Athaliah, was given to Joram of Judah, a son of Jehoshaphat, to cement the new good relations between the two countries that had a common past in the tribal nation Israel. Jehoshaphat and Ahab together made war against Damascus to recover Transjordan, an occupied area in which both had territorial interests (1 Kings 22). Traditionally, both Judah and Israel had control over Transjordanian lands. The same anti-Aramaean alliance was continued by Ahaziah, son of Joram and Athaliah, and Joram of Israel, a son or grandson of Ahab (2 Kings 8:28-29).

The whole of the Omride measures was very successful in strengthening Israel, so much so that in the anti-Assyrian coalition, which was able to stop the Assyrian army at Qarqar, Ahab was one of the three leaders along with the kings of Damascus and of Hamath. He brought to that combat a force of two thousand chariots and ten thousand foot soldiers, according to the documents of Salmanezer III of Assyria.

The major problems the Omrides had to face came from within the nation. It was not possible for Yahweh to live peacefully alongside Baal. Yahweh was a jealous God (Exod. 34:14-17) who would not tolerate that the people should have other gods alongside Yahweh. This characteristic feature of Yahweh is due to the revolutionary struggle that the tribes had engaged against the Canaanite cities, which were presided over by other gods who legitimated domination. The political strategy of Omri and his descendents was probably one of establishing an official Baal cult in the capital Samaria without interfering with the Yahweh sanctuaries in Bethel and Dan. Baal would be the god of Samaria and Yahweh the God of the tribes.

This could not work. The prophet Elijah challenged the whole people in these terms: "How long will you limp on both feet? If Yahweh is God, follow Yahweh; if Baal, follow Baal" (1 Kings 18:21). Bloody conflicts followed. Jezabel is said to have "wiped out" the prophets of Yahweh (1 Kings 18:4). Elijah is said to have decapitated the prophets of Baal (1 Kings 18:40). The truth is that there were bloody conflicts between the followers of Yahweh and the followers of Baal. Peaceful coexistence was not possible.

The story of Naboth's vineyard (1 Kings 21) allows us to see how much was at stake for ordinary people in this conflict, which was apparently religious. King Ahab coveted the ancestral vineyard of Naboth which happened to be next to the royal residence in Jezreel, much to the misfortune of Naboth. Appealing to the Sinaitic laws that forbade the estrangement of productive lands (Lev. 25:23-31), Naboth refused to sell the vineyard and the king had no alternative: He had to accept the justice of Naboth's decision, supported as it was by Israel's laws. But Jezabel, who knew from the political traditions of her land that there was no law above the will of a king proceeded to "confiscate" Naboth's vineyard (1 Kings 21:4-16). Here we see the social reasons for the conflict between Yahweh and Baal. At stake were the economic interests of the Israelites, whose very subsistence depended on their lands, which were protected by the laws of Yahweh (and not by the religious traditions of Baal).

The leaders of the opposition were Elijah and, after his death, his disciple Elisha, both prophets of Yahweh. They prepared the conditions for the downfall of the Omrides in the year 841 B.C.E.

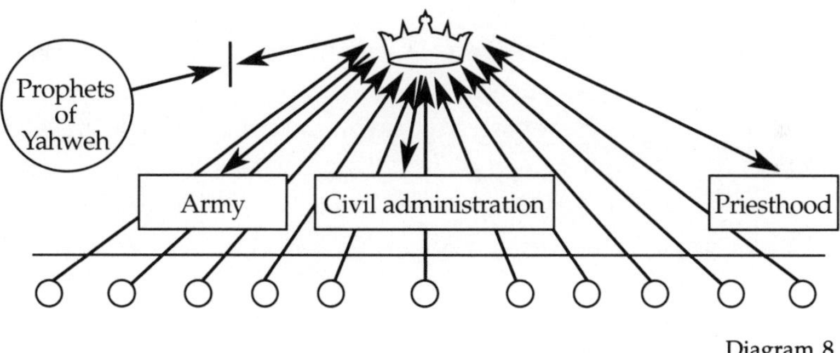

Diagram 8

This diagram represents more the political intentions of Omri and his descendents than the facts. Their intentions were to establish in Israel a society on the Canaanite model, preserving Yahwism as a purely religious ornament. The same scheme of society had existed in Egypt against which Moses and his followers rebelled. They did not think it necessary to eliminate the cult of Yahweh, but rather left it as a people's religion alongside the official worship, which was rendered to Baal in Samaria. This became impossible because the prophets could not tolerate an arrangement that left liberty for a Yahweh cult on the condition that it not affect the structures of domination. The texts suggest that it was Jezabel who initiated the religious persecution, however, it seems more likely that it was the prophets of Yahweh who first rejected the proposal. Baal had no reason to fight Yahweh; Yahweh had every reason to fight Baal as a religious legitimation for the oppression of the people of Yahweh. This floating circle of prophets of Yahweh did not accept staying out of politics, rather they entered into conflict with the official religious administration.

We are poorly informed about the village organization, but it seems natural to suppose that the tribes continued to exist and that, for this reason, it was not possible to establish stable channels for directly collecting the tribute of the peasants to support the state apparatus.

6
Religious Fervor and Excess in the Dynasty of Jehu 841-752 B.C.E.

The dynasty of Omri ended in 841 B.C.E. with an uprising from within the army, in a similar fashion to the end of the dynasties of Jeroboam and Baasha. As in the two former cases, it is probable that the sector of the army that protagonized the military coup was sensitive to the frustrations of the people of Israel. It was their intention to end the tyranny of kings who did not consider the welfare of the people and did not respect the legal traditions that were the defense of the rights of the poor.

The coup was headed by a certain Jehu, an officer in the army that was fighting against Aram in Transjordan. It was an extraordinarily bloody coup. King Joram was, naturally, assassinated (2 Kings 9:22-26), as were his mother (2 Kings 9:30-37) and his seventy sons (2 Kings 10:1-11). The king of Judah, Ahaziah, who happened to be in Israel, possibly to support the war against Aram, was also killed (2 Kings 9:27-29). This Ahaziah was the son of Athaliah, the daughter of Ahab who had married the Judahite king. A whole group of the Judahite royal family died also (2 Kings 10:12-14).

Just as religion had played an important role in the attempt of Omri and his house to strengthen the state, it also played an important role in his downfall. The biblical text emphasizes that the uprising of Jehu was because of the incitement of the prophet Elisha (2 Kings 9:1-10), and sees it as the culmination of the prophecies of Elijah against Ahab (2 Kings 9:25-26, 36). For reasons we have already explored we can be sure that the hostility of the prophets of Yahweh against the Omrides was very deep and that their participation in his overthrow was enthusiastic.

Second Kings give much importance to the religious measures undertaken by Jehu to wipe out the cult of Baal in Samaria (2 Kings 10:18-27). He killed not only the priests and the prophets of Baal, but also purged all of those whom he could identify as followers of Baal.

The historians of Kings, with their well-known Jerusalemite bias, or rather, in spite of this bias, say, "Jehu wiped out Baal from Israel" (2 Kings 10:28). This surprising affirmation cannot be taken at face value. Jehu wiped out the official Baal cult in the capital city and desecrated the temple which the kings had built there. But Baal was also a god to many peasants because of Baal's identification with rain. Joash, father of Gideon, in the heroic tribal period had kept a sanctuary of Baal on his property (Judg. 6:25), and for this reason was not regarded as a full Israelite. We may suppose that the clandestine or private worship of Baal among the peasants was widely extended. It would have facilitated the introduction of Baal in Samaria, but it was something different. Jehu, then, eliminated the official cult of Baal from Israel, although there is no evidence that he tried to wipe out the more private cult of Baal.

Immediately after informing about the elimination of the cult of Baal, the historians add their customary assessment, "but Jehu did not turn aside from the sins with which Jeroboam the son of Nebat caused Israel to sin, the bulls of Bethel and Dan" (2 Kings 10:29). This confirms our interpretation of the religious policy of Jeroboam, that it was not with the intention of drawing Israel away from Yahweh but from the Temple of Jerusalem. This was enough for the historians who wrote the books of the Kings to condemn him. From the perspective of the poor this is not so, and we must take distance from these judgments of the historians who did not have the poor as their major concern.

As one would expect, the deaths in the royal family of Judah during this coup d'etat in Israel destroyed the alliance between the two countries. This problem was compounded by internal disputes in Jerusalem. War did not actually break out for fifty years, when Amaziah, king of Judah, attacked Joash of Israel. He had overestimated his strength and suffered a sound defeat, including his own captivity in Samaria (2 Kings 14:8-14).

This victory over Judah is only one reflection of the strength that the house of Jehu was able to build in Israel. After a series of military reverses under Jehu himself (2 Kings 10:32-33), which continued during the days of his son Jehoahaz (2 Kings 13:22), Joash was able to reverse this trend and to recover lost territories (2 Kings 13:24-25). Jeroboam, the son of Joash, enjoyed a long and prosperous reign (792–752) B.C.E. and even some territorial expansion (2 Kings 14:25). Archaeological excavations among the ruins of the period confirm the high level of prosperity achieved during Jeroboam's reign, although accompanied by an increased disparity in life-styles between rich and poor.

In order to understand the structuring of Israelite society under Jehu and his descendents, the function of religion continues to be decisive. Jehu returned the traditional sanctuaries of Yahweh worship to their former prominence, among which Bethel was the most important. Dan had probably lost most of its significance because of its geographical location in a border area where Israelite dominion was not stable.

Jehu had to decide what to do with Omri's capital Samaria which was a royal city after the Canaanite pattern. After desecrating its temple and killing those who had worked within the political order established by Omri with its Baal cult, the city must have been left in a shambles with very little population. Our texts show no interest in the measures Jehu must have taken to repopulate the city, but he must have done so, because it was not abandoned. In the later history of Jehuite Israel Samaria continued being the capital. It is certain that with this royal city for a capital the kings were able to maintain a much stronger state than that of the first Jeroboam, so that the dynasty of Jehu does not represent a simple restoration of the kingdom prior to the Omrides. As a consequence of the unfortunate experience of forty years of a Baalistic state Israel emerged stronger than before.

In spite of this, Jehu was not able to construct a temple of Yahweh in Samaria, as we might have expected. Probably the importance of the group around Elijah and Elisha within Jehu's "political party" served as an insuperable obstacle to any such ideas Jehu may have harbored. They wished to restore a kingdom in which the prophets were autonomous over against the kings, with the capacity to withdraw their support when they understood this to be the will of Yahweh. We can represent Israel during this period (841–752 B.C.E.) in the following fashion:

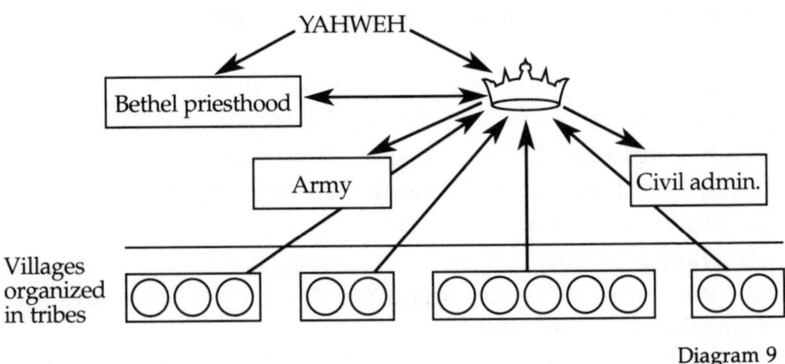

Diagram 9

The tribal organization continued to offer a certain defense to the Israelite peasants. The prophet Amos still spoke at this time of the judicial function of the elders, for example (Amos 5:15, "the gate" is the place of reunion of the elders). The army may have kept its ties to the tribes. Between 752 and 722, when Samaria was destroyed, there were three more military coups, but with all certainty the civil bureaucracy with its center in the city of Samaria grew and the tributes to support it also grew. The merchants about whose abuses Amos is so eloquent may have been state functionaries, although it is also possible that they were free economic agents (Amos 8:4-8).

The most important priesthood of Yahweh was that at Bethel, which continued to be the principal national sanctuary. It had close ties to the crown (Amos 7:10-17). The Bethel priests were indebted to the kings for having restored them after the persecution they had suffered during the Omri dynasty, but the fact that not the least trace of a royal theology has survived from Bethel indicates that they were not servants in the employ of the kings. Religion kept some independence, although we are not well informed. The absence of native prophets during the next hundred years, or at least the absence of reports of prophets, makes us suspect that things were not well for a vigorous tradition of Yahweh the Liberator. The tradition appears quiescent.

A prophet from Judah arrived at Bethel during the latter years of the reign of Jeroboam II to assume the mantle of Elijah and other distinguished predecessors. Amos prophesied in Bethel and there made a profound analysis of the injustices that gave the lie to the official profession of faith in Yahweh, the God of the Exodus.

There was luxury in Samaria and a lack of concern for the misery of the general population (Amos 6:1-7; 3:13-15; 4:1-3). Merchants sold shoddy goods at exorbitant prices, thus earning profit on the need of the people (Amos 8:4-8; 2:6). The elders themselves twisted the law in the judgment gatherings (5:10-12; 5:15). All of this went along with an enthusiastic and superficially orthodox worship (Amos 4:4-5; 5:21-24).

Yet, precisely because Yahweh had a privileged relationship with the people Yahweh had brought out of slavery in Egypt, Yahweh would be firm in demanding account of their sin (Amos 3:1-2). They would be destroyed without any remnant (Amos 9:1-4), and if any thought that Yahweh would not destroy Yahweh's people, let that person know that Yahweh could just as well take the Philistines or the Syrians and make them the beneficiaries of Yahweh's saving actions (Amos 9:7).

These were strong words, and yet, Amos did not have a positive proposal to transform national life. He did not seek to remove Jeroboam from being king. Perhaps this was because he was a foreigner, even though he shared the religious traditions of Israel. He was content to make his condemnation without a proposal for redemption.

Some years after Amos the last great prophet of the kingdom of Israel arose, Hosea. For this prophet the very existence of a monarchy in Israel was a grievous problem, a manifestation of a much deeper problem, the unbridled search for material things. Yahweh, the Savior God whom Israel had known since the Exodus, continued to be recognized as the national God, but the search for material things had made Yahweh into a Baal, a god of rain and fertility, a giver of abundance. The people claimed to know God, but their rejection of what is good and right gave them the lie (Hos. 8:1-3).

Hosea's wife had been a whore (Hos. 1:2) and he considered prostitution a good image for national life. The life of Israel was a constant search for wheat, oil, silver, wool, and linen, without considering that a stable provision of these needs of life comes from keeping justice within a community of reverence for Yahweh (Hos. 2:10-11 [2:8-9]). In order to satisfy their appetite they filled the land with lies, murder, and robbery, proving thereby that there was no real knowledge of God (Hos. 4:1-3). Even should they repent with pious prayers, Yahweh, who wants love and not sacrifices, would pay no attention to them (Hos. 5:15—6:6).

The kings were a manifestation of this deep wrong, for the evil of Israel could be traced back to Gilgal, where Samuel anointed Saul, the first king (Hos. 9:15), and its injustices derived from Gibeah, the home village of Saul (Hos. 10:9). In the day of their misfortune the kings, which the people had demanded without taking Yahweh into account, would prove of no help (Hos. 8:4; 13:9-11).

As a result of this prostituted life, Israel as a state would have to cease, in Hosea's opinion. Yahweh would call the nation to the desert and make a new alliance there in justice, right, love, and fidelity (Hos. 2:16, 21-22 [2:14, 19-20]). For this new future, the prophet believed that there would be a restoration of the original unity of Israel and Judah (Hos. 2:1-3 [1:10—2:1]) under the leadership one "head" (significantly, not a king). The message was one of a return to the national roots. Turning to Egypt or Assyria would be no help, for the true strength of the nation would have to be found in its own roots; hence, the emphasis on the original Yahweh of the Exodus and the recovery of the political necessity of the unity of the two states that drew on the Exodus traditions.

7
Judah, the Davidic Redoubt 931-722 B.C.E.

During these two centuries between the rebellion of the tribes against the house of David (931 B.C.E.) and the destruction of Samaria (722 B.C.E.) a small Davidic state was able to maintain itself apart from Israel, which had previously been the tribe of Judah and at this time became the kingdom of Judah. Jerusalem, the City of David, did not join the rebellion of the tribes and was able to keep control over the tribe of Judah and part of that of Benjamin. Jerusalem and its surrounding lands were in a more or less isolated location in mountains that were not on any commercial route. This meant that it was not the object of the covetousness of merchants and stronger nations. In other words, it enjoyed a beneficent neglect on the part of its neighbors.

With the annexation of the territory of Israel into the Assyrian Empire in the late eighth century, to be discussed later, and the forced exile of its leaders after the fall of Samaria (722), Judah was left as the sole historical link with the revolutionary experience of the tribes of Israel. It is this accident of history that gives Jerusalem and Judah the importance they have within the Bible.

To put this situation in perspective it helps to compare the books of Kings with Chronicles. Both describe the history of the kings. Kings, which were composed toward the end of the history of Judah at the end of the seventh century and the beginning of the sixth, are part of a great historical work that begins with Moses and ends with the destruction of Jerusalem. This is what exegetes know as the Deuteronomistic History (Dtr), which begins with Deuteronomy and includes Joshua, Judges, the two books of Samuel and the two books of Kings. For the period that concerns us, 931 to 722 B.C.E., Kings rightly give priority to Israel over Judah in their historical account, reflecting where the greater political power lay and where the greater continuity with the tribal origins remained. This history is written, however, in the shadow of the destruction of Samaria in order to prepare its readers and hearers (books were normally read aloud to groups of listeners) to understand this event. It was also written out of the theological need to justify the action of Yahweh in destroying Israel while leaving Judah untouched. The grave sin of Israel, according to these historians, was Jeroboam's sin in separating Israel from the Temple at Jerusalem. We have already noted that this judgment does not reflect the interests of the poor peasants of Israel or Judah.

Chronicles (or Paralipomena) tell the same history except that they begin it with David, ending as Kings do with the destruction of Jerusalem. The history is prepared with an extensive list of genealogies (lists of families), which begin with Adam (1 Chronicles 1–9). For the history proper they omit almost everything that has to do with the kingdom of Israel. This is the history of Judah presented as the true Israel and of Jerusalem as the holy city. The kingdom of Israel is considered an apostate kingdom from its beginnings for rebelling against David, Yahweh's chosen one (read Abijah's speech in 2 Chron. 13.4-12, which is very instructive for the Chronicler's theological perspective on Israel). This is the victors' point of view (or the survivors') on history. When we want to read the Bible from the point of view of the poor we must read this kind of literature critically. It can provide us with valuable historical information, but its perspective is theologically alien to the interests of the poor.

When in 931 B.C.E. the tribes rose up against young King Rehoboam, he was able to take refuge in Jerusalem, a walled city most of whose inhabitants were his "servants," the administrators of the kingdom. From Jerusalem he and his descendents were able to set up a kingdom separate from Israel, which continued the political and religious traditions of David. For an army he still had the elite palace troop and the troops of the tribes of Judah and Benjamin. As civil administrators he had a very large body, the personnel who had administered the great extensions that David conquered. Many of the royal administrators whom David and Solomon had put over the tribes of Israel, the governors of the districts and their employees, fled and sought refuge in Jerusalem and Judah with Rehoboam. He then had a surplus of able administrators, and the personnel of the Temple of Jerusalem were the most loyal of his followers. For them Yahweh had chosen David and his descendants to rule the people of Israel, and the uprising of the tribes could only be understood as rebellion against the will of Yahweh.

What existed in Jerusalem at that time was a classic tributary society under the personal control of the king:

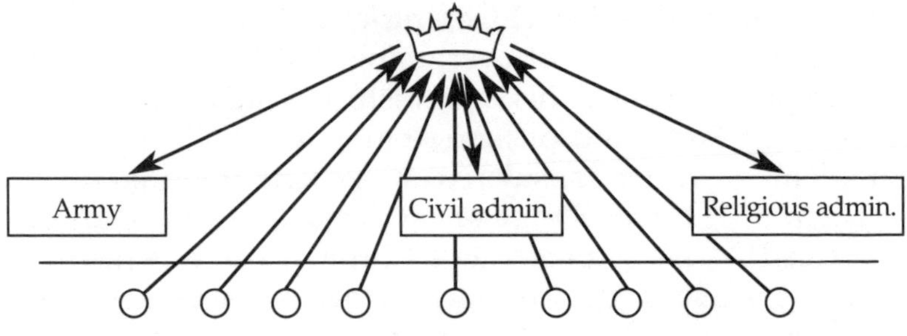

Diagram 10

During the reigns of Rehoboam (931–913 B.C.E.), Abijam (913–911), and Asa (911–870) there were wars with Israel apparently caused by the Judahite pressures to push its borders to the north. In the time of Jehoshaphat (873–848 B.C.E.) peace was reached with Israel, a peace that was cemented by the marriage of his son Joram to Athaliah, a daughter of Ahab. Israel and Judah were then allies in war against Aram in an effort to regain the region of Transjordan.

The peace with Israel was abruptly ended with the death of most of the royal family at the hands of Jehu during the coup d'etat of 841 B.C.E. Athaliah, the mother of the murdered king Ahaziah and herself a member of the royal family that Jehu wiped out in Israel, was left alone on the throne of Judah. Athaliah was overthrown a few years later by a coalition of priests and of "the people of the land," that is, the principal men of the provincial cities (2 Kings 11). Noteworthy in this list of those who removed the queen mother from the throne is the absence of the royal administrative personnel of Jerusalem. "So all the people of the land rejoiced, but the city was quiet after Athaliah had been killed with the sword at the king's house" (1 Kings 11:20). Joash, son of Ahaziah and grandson of Athaliah, was placed on the throne. This Joash had a long reign (835–797), until he was assassinated by an attempted coup of his "servants." His son Amaziah succeeded to the throne, but his reign ended unfortunately when he was taken captive by the Israelite army during an ill-advised war he launched against Israel. His reign covered the years 797–768, including an undefined number of years of captivity during which his son was the king in Jerusalem (2 Kings 14:8-14). At this time, the Israelite army broke down the walls around Jerusalem. This war took place in 791 B.C.E. For a long period afterward, dominated by the long reigns of Azariah (Uzziah) in Judah (792–740, beginning with a coregency even before his father's captivity in Israel) and Jeroboam in Israel (793–753), there was peace between Israel and Judah.

In order to understand the dynamics of political life in Judah it is necessary to look at what Kings say about the many political difficulties of the ninth century. Ahaziah was assassinated in the year 841 for reasons internal to Israel's politics rather than those of his own country Judah. The effect was to bring his mother to power, who had the support of the palace personnel, but she encountered the opposition of the traditional Yahwistic priests because she had established a temple of Baal with the support of the royal court. A coalition was formed against her, headed by the Yahwistic priests of the Jerusalem Temple and the "people of the land," with the support of part of the army. In 835 she was deposed and assassinated after six years of her reign, her Baal temple destroyed, and her grandson Joash installed on the throne (2 Kings 11:1-20).

During his long reign, Joash entered into conflict with the priests who apparently failed to obey royal orders to repair the Temple, preferring to spend the money (2 Kings 12:5-17). The servants of the king, with the support of the priests this time, had him killed in 797. Nevertheless, Joash's son Amaziah was able to succeed him. Amaziah's reign, as we saw, was interrupted in 791 by his captivity in Israel following a disastrous war. After he was freed at an undetermined date some years later, he was murdered by the Jerusalem servants. This was in 768, probably shortly after his release (2 Kings 14:18-21). The text does not explain the reasons for this murder; it is understandable that his sudden return to the throne after over twelve years of absence, during which his son had been the sole ruler, would have upset the palace routine.

Putting all this information together we discover that there were ongoing tensions between the kings and their own state personnel in Jerusalem. We can explain this as due to the inflated state bureaucracy and a tributary base that was too small to sustain it. The state apparatus must have been the source of the expansionist pressures that carried Judah to such an aggressive foreign policy. The problem seems to have been greatest among the civil administrators. It was easier to reduce the army to a size that accorded with the reduced dimensions of Judah after the revolt of the tribes of Israel. The priesthood had a vested interest in the stability of the Davidic dynasty by reason of the Davidic theology it taught and practiced.

The greatest strength of the support for the Davidic house was the "people of the land," the powerful men of the provincial cities. During the whole period of Judah's history they supported administrative reforms to reduce the state personnel and to concentrate it in the capital city. The first effort in this direction was made early in Judah's history under King Asa (911–870 B.C.E.): Asa "removed from all the cities of Judah the high places and incense altars" (2 Chron. 14:4), places that were not just centers of worship but also government agencies.

More important were the administrative reforms of Jehoshaphat (873–848 B.C.E.; 2 Chron. 17:6), and more than a century later Hezekiah (716–687) carried out the deepest reforms of all. He carried forth a thorough centralizing of state functions—civil and religious—in the city of Jerusalem (2 Chronicles 29–31). This centralization left the field outside of Jerusalem to the "people of the land," in exchange for the decided support that they gave to the Davidic kings.

8
The Prophets of the Late Eighth Century in Judah

After the fall of the kingdom of Israel, where an important number of prophets of Yahweh had arisen, prophets arose for the first time in Judah. In the days of Hezekiah there were two great Judahite prophets of very different tendencies, one from the capital and the other from the countryside. Both attempted to analyze the situation of Judah, which by this time was the only heir of the tribes of Israel. Their analyses are quite different and allow us to understand the complexities of faith in this real world where things are not always black and white.

Isaiah was from Jerusalem, where he saw a vision of Yahweh in the Temple (Isa. 6). After seeing this vision he assumed the role of a prophet, a role critical of the kings of his time. He denounced those who accumulated land in the country (Isa. 5:8). He also denounced those rulers, judges, and others, who did not do justice to the weak (Isa. 10:4). He found it especially disgusting that the leaders should pose as pious and religious people, devoted to Yahweh, while they lived from the exploitation of the people (Isa. 1:10-17).

Isaiah was different from earlier prophets of whom we are informed because he made his theoretical framework the Davidic theology and not the Exodus. He accepted the doctrine that Jerusalem was a privileged city in Yahweh's eyes, and a place where the poor could find protection (Isa. 14:28-32), and he clung to this conviction, in spite of the fact that in his time Jerusalem had become a refuge for murderers. He believed that Yahweh would purify the city as silver is cleansed by fire of its dross; it would again become the city of justice it was destined to be (Isa. 1:21-26).

The hope for the people of Israel (Judah), according to Isaiah, is the emergence of a good king, the anointed one (or Messiah, a technical term for the future good king, which we owe to Isaiah). Isaiah issued at least three important messianic oracles (Isa. 9:1-6; 11:1-9; and 32:1-5, 15-20). In these sayings one can see how it was possible within the confines of the Davidic theology to denounce injustice and announce hope. In the Jerusalem cult known to Isaiah it was declared that the king will bring justice to the poor, as we can see in a royal psalm like Psalm 72, but the kings of Isaiah's time, Ahaz and Hezekiah, either could not or would not control the abuses of their officials who lived off the goods of the poor. The prophet Isaiah announces that they shall be like a tree which is cut down (Isa. 6:13). Yet, from the stump of the tree a shoot will grow, a truly good king who will defend the humble people (Isa. 11:1-9).

Isaiah was not, then, as radical as Hosea for whom the institution of monarchy was sinful in itself. For Isaiah the evil is not in the family of David nor in the monarchic institution but in the evil kings that Judah has to endure. Nevertheless, Yahweh will raise a good king who will be the salvation of the people. From the viewpoint of the poor, this analysis seems not quite enough. Isaiah does not even imagine that the people might organize themselves to achieve their goals. The welfare of the people will be achieved by means of a messianic benefactor. Perhaps it is our longer historical experience that makes us in the twentieth century sense that this is a formula for tyranny, however well meaning the prophet may have been. Paternalistic rulers who see popular welfare as only possible as a result of their own generosity often become the worst of tyrants.

Micah was a prophet of peasant origins. As he saw things in Judah, the rulers were devouring the flesh of the people (Mic. 3:1-4). Jerusalem as a city was built with the blood of the people, and there the rulers, priests, and prophets alike were thieves (Mic. 3:9-12). Sin was not just the result of evil persons; it was structural. The very existence of Jerusalem was the sin of Judah (Mic. 1:5, following the LXX), a truly remarkable analysis!

This being Micah's assessment of the situation of the nation, he could not expect any hope out of a future purification of the city. The only solution for Yahweh's people was that the city be destroyed, including especially the Temple that consecrated the situation of structural evil (Mic. 3:12).

The effects of the exploitation by the city were felt in the countryside. Powerful men, most of whom lived in the city or had their power base there, took the lands of the peasants for themselves (Mic. 2:1-3).

The solution Micah proposes is a peasant revolution to recover the lands. "My people rises as an enemy" (Mic. 2:8 following the Hebrew; all translations in current use change the sense of the sentence). "Cast out the rulers (following LXX; MT has 'women' instead of 'rulers') of my people from their pleasure homes" (Mic. 2:9). "Arise! Move forward! This is not a time to rest!" (Mic. 2:10). These are revolutionary calls, although both MT and LXX show the corruption resulting from the work of scribes who tried to soften them, and modern translators in general fail to see through their camouflage.

There will be an assembly of Yahweh to distribute anew the land, as was done in the days of Joshua (Joshua 14–19). There the landlords will wail that they have been despoiled, because they shall have no part in the distribution of lands (Mic. 2:4-5).

For Micah the social problem of Judah was not limited to the house of David, that is, to the kings and the city of the kings. In a saying that is hard to understand in its details because it is built on puns and alliteration (Mic. 1:10-16), the prophet calls for the destruction of the provincial cities of Judah, cities like Lachish, Akzib, and Gath. Probably it was cities such as these that were the power base of the "people of the land" who had proved such a firm support for the house of David. It was in these cities where the landlords lived who had stolen the lands of the peasants. It does not seem too risky to suppose that the landlords and the "people of the land" were one and the same.

Micah is the most radical people's prophet in the Bible because he understands that Yahweh will not work the liberation of the people without the organized action of the people themselves. The people must understand that the Jerusalem Temple, the Davidic kings, and the grand lords of the provincial cities, are all their oppressors. They will have to dare in the name of Yahweh of the Exodus to destroy the Temple of which the priests claim that it is the dwelling of Yahweh and even to kill the kings of whom the priests say that Yahweh has chosen them to "pastor" the people. This is truly a return to the revolutionary God of Moses!

In reading the book of Micah it is absolutely necessary to take note that his words were modified so as to not cause offense to later readers. The prophet's words, almost all of which are found in the first three chapters, were embellished with other prophetic sayings that were not revolutionary in order to give an overall impression that is not radical. To read the Bible from the viewpoint of the poor is here as elsewhere to look in the text for the struggles of the poor and also to look for their oppression by the powerful. This struggle is present in the Bible itself, a book of the people that has been appropriated and twisted by the oppressors of the poor. Even so, in a prophet like Micah we again find the presence of the God who liberates the poor, the God who lifted up a Moses to lead God's people to freedom.

9
Palestine under Assyrian Domination 738-630 B.C.E.

The Imperial Expansion

With the warrior king Tiglath-Pileser III (745–727 B.C.E.), Assyria made it a priority to achieve control over the whole of the land access to Egypt. This meant first of all to dominate the coastal route that went through Phoenicia and Philistia. To assure control over this route it was necessary from the viewpoint of the empire to have friendly regimes in the hills of Palestine where the kingdoms of Israel and Judah were situated. During a long period, the successive Assyrian kings made frequent incursions into Palestine, reaching their greatest extent in 663 B.C.E. under Assurbanipal, when they entered Egypt and were able to sack the capital city Thebes.

Tiglath-Pileser III made his first campaign into Palestine in 738 B.C.E.. He entered the north through Syria and reached Phoenicia where he established a province with its capital in Simirra on the coastal plain. Israel had not been touched yet. His second campaign, in 734, began the dismembering of Israel. Tiglath-Pileser came down the coast as far as the Philistine city of Gaza. Apparently, it was on the coastal plain that he met and defeated the army of Israel. As a result he annexed to the Assyrian Empire Dor (on the coastland), Meguiddo (including all the hills of Galilee), and Gilead (Transjordan) as provinces. Israel was reduced to the hills of Ephraim where the capital city Samaria was located. This happened during the reign of Pekah, and the Bible informs us briefly about this catastrophe (2 Kings 15:29).

In 722 B.C.E., under King Sargon II, the city of Samaria was taken after a siege, and was subsequently converted into the head of another province. As the final result of Assyrian expansion Israel was divided into four Assyrian provinces. Meanwhile, Judah had been made into a satellite that rendered tribute to Assyria and was submissive to Assyrian foreign policy. This happened during the reign of Ahaz (735–716). In this same year the Philistine city of Ashdod was also made into a satellite kingdom.

Sargon II made a new incursion into Palestine in 720, going as far as the "River of Egypt" where he destroyed the city of Rapihu, on the Palestinian border with Egypt. In his next expedition in 716 he brought people from the east to repopulate the city because of its strategic value. Returning in 711, he suppressed the kingdom of Ashdod and turned it into a province, although he allowed the Philistine cities of Ekron and Ashkelon to keep the status of subject kingdoms, as also Gaza to the south.

The definitive configuration of Assyrian Palestine was achieved with the campaign of Sennacherib in 701 B.C.E. The Assyrian army defeated the army of Judah led by Hezekiah at the fortress city of Lachish, which protected the Judahite flank against the Philistines to the west. Sennacherib separated Jerusalem from both the cities and territory of the hills of Judah, and from the foothills that descend toward the Mediterranean Sea. As the vassal kingdom of Judah all that was left was Jerusalem and its immediate environs. The rest of what had been the kingdom of Judah was divided among the Philistine vassal kingdoms of Ekron, Ashkelon, and Gaza. This happened during the reign of Hezekiah (716–687 B.C.E.).

It is probable that during the long reign of Manasseh in Judah (697–642, a coregency with his father for the first ten years) much of these territories were recovered, not by means of war, but through negotiations with the empire. Nevertheless, at the time of the fall of Samaria in 722, Israel was totally incorporated into Assyria, and Judah after 734 escaped the same fate only by submitting as a vassal kingdom whose margin of independence was reduced progressively until only the capital was left after Sennacherib's campaign of 701.

Internal Political History

The dynasty of Jehu, which had purified Israel of the cult of Baal, ended in 752 B.C.E. when the king Zechariah was murdered by Shallum. A month later Menahem challenged Shallum and was able to install himself as king in Samaria from 752 until 742. He paid a heavy tribute to Tiglath-Pileser in order not to have problems with the empire (2 Kings 15:19-20). It appears from surviving data, which is in a confused state, that Gilead was controlled by a different king whose name was Pekah. In 740, Pekah with a small contingent of men from Gilead, managed to kill Pekahiah, the son of Menahem, and make himself king in Samaria (2 Kings 15:25). He attempted a policy of political independence from Assyria with the consequence of a disastrous defeat at the hands of Tiglath-Pileser III in 734 and the loss of the plain (Dor), Galilee (the province of Meguiddo), and Gilead, as we have seen.

To complete the picture we must understand the war between Israel and Judah in 734. Jotham, king of Judah (750–732), had some success in realizing the old claims of Judah in Transjordan, for he was able to defeat the Ammonites there (2 Chron. 27:5). Pekah of Israel and Rezin of Damascus as a reaction to these Judahite successes and in an attempt to create a united front against Assyria supported the claims of a certain Tobias (= Tabel in Isa. 7:6) to the throne of Judah. This Tobias was probably an ancestor of the lineage of the "Ammonite" Tobiases who made problems for Nehemiah the governor of Judea some three centuries later (Neh. 2:19; 4:1; 13:4; and so on). To protect himself Ahaz the Judahite king voluntarily submitted to Tiglath-Pileser, thus complicating Palestinian political life.

The failures of the policies of independence of Pekah exposed him to a conspiracy from a certain Hosea, son of Elah, who killed him in the year 732, thereafter announcing himself the vassal of Assyria (2 Kings 17:3). When he conspired with the king "So" of Egypt a few years later, he became the victim of Assyrian vengeance, falling along with the entire kingdom of Israel, as we have said earlier, in 722 B.C.E. (2 Kings 17:4-6).

During its last thirty years (752–722), Israel experienced three coups d'etat. Two of them were pro-Assyrian (Menahem and Hosea) and the other one, between the two, was anti-Assyrian (Pekah). Coups were in themselves nothing new in Israel's national experience. Baasha, Omri, and Jehu had attained the throne by means of military coups and been able to establish stable reigns. However, in these cases the military action followed upon the intervention of a prophet of Yahweh, which had the effect of undermining the legitimacy of the reigning king and could, hence, be seen as the just actions of Yahweh in defense of the poor. Even more, Jeroboam and Jehu were recognized by the prophets Shemaiah and Elisha, respectively, even before they took power. These latter coups were different. The prophet Hosea spoke of them in the following terms:

> They have made kings with taking me into account, and have made princes without my knowledge. (Hos. 8:4)
>
> Where is, then, your king, that he may save you, and your judges in all your cities—those of whom you said, "Give me a king and princes"? A king in my anger I give, and I take him back in my fury. (Hos. 13:10-11)

According to the same prophet, the life of Israel at this time can be understood as the life of a whore, a woman who abandons the norms of social life in order to pursue material goods (Hos. 2:4-17). While this situation persists, religion will be of no avail: "They cry out: My God, we in Israel know you! But Israel has rejected the good: The enemy will pursue!" (Hos. 8:2-3). The evidence that there is no true knowledge of God in spite of the abundance of religious practices is the multiplication of lies and robbery in the wild pursuit of well-being and material goods (Hos. 4:1-3).

One of the practices of the Assyrian Empire, once it took the step of incorporating a vassal kingdom as an Assyrian province, was to undertake important population displacements. That is, besides displacing the native king and replacing him with an Assyrian governor, they also carried out ample movements of the leading members of the subject society, exchanging them with the elites removed from distant provinces. This practice is documented in Assyrian inscriptions and the biblical texts affirm that it was carried out with Israel (2 Kings 15:29; 17:24). The purpose of these movements was to break up the national life by placing in the major cities a population with different language and customs from those of the peasant hinterland on which they would depend for their daily sustenance.

In a sense the provinces continued being part of the great Judahite-Israelite community, so that the famous question about the ten lost tribes is false from the outset because it wrongly supposes that whole tribal populations were removed. Those who disappeared from history were only the urban residents displaced by the Assyrians to new areas where they were presumably integrated into the local population. The peasant population kept faith with its religious culture and served as the population base for later Galilean Judaism and Samaritan Judaism.

Unfortunately we have no documents that would allow us to evaluate the quality of the life of the peasants in these Assyrian provinces. It is possible that economically life went on much as before during the century in which Amos and Hosea show that their fate was not at all good, and it is probable that politically the peace and tranquility of existence in the Assyrian province would have proved preferable to the frequent wars with their sequel of death and misery during the period of independence. Nevertheless, the loss of a national cultural life, where the cities and their sanctuaries had played a major role, must have been felt as a real loss.

Judah as the Heir of Israel

With the incorporation into the Assyrian Empire of what had been Israel, Judah was left as a vassal kingdom with the sole inheritance of the national identity of the people who knew themselves as the people of Yahweh. The presence of traditions from Israel in the literature that was written in Judah is sufficient witness that not all of the cultural leaders of Israel were deported: Some emigrated to Judah, fleeing from the Assyrians, and embraced Judah as the true Israel. Instead of pining over the loss of the ancient sanctuaries like Bethel, Gilgal, Dan, and Beersheba, Jerusalem imposed itself as the norm and its Temple as the only place where Yahweh wished to receive sacrifices. A new reading of the Yahwist tradition had to be made. In that new reading the royal Davidic ideology of Jerusalem, which was alien and probably offensive to Israelites, was reduced. From the resulting faith it was possible to build something that would be attractive to the Israelites who now lived in the Assyrian provinces and who, previously, had not accepted the Jerusalem Temple as a legitimate Yahweh sanctuary. At some time pilgrimages from the Assyrian provinces began in order to celebrate the feasts of Yahweh in Jerusalem. It is in this context that we are to understand the considerable literary activity of the late Assyrian period.

Among the sayings of Hosea there is one, probably authentic, which visualizes a day in which "the sons of Judah and the sons of Israel will join in one, will name one head (*rosh*), and will spread out over the land, because it will be the great day of Jezreel" (Hos. 2:2). That is to say, even before Samaria was taken, Hosea felt that the future of Israel lay in a union with Judah. It is noteworthy that he does not speak of a "king" as the leader of the two nations, and he probably did not think of a king. The book of Hosea underwent a Judahite redaction, which can be seen in the few allusions that announce, among other things, that "the sons of Israel will return; they will seek Yahweh their God *and David their king*" (Hos. 3:5).

Amos had announced the total destruction of Israel (Amos 9:1-4). With the passage of time the book of this prophet suffered some additions to assure that Israel would return to David (Amos 9:11-15).

The Judahite King Hezekiah (716–687 B.C.E.) reacted officially to the new situation in which he found himself as the only king who was the heir to the ancient traditions of Israel. He carried out a purification of the religious practices in his kingdom, eliminating not only the cults of foreign gods but also destroying all places of worship except Jerusalem (2 Kings 18:1-6). Within the Temple of Jerusalem he destroyed the bronze serpent, which it was believed had been made by Moses in the desert. Interpreters debate the meaning of these measures. It does not seem difficult to understand that, with the purpose of giving to Jerusalem a dimension that went beyond what was Judahite, he should seek to exalt its dignity, even at the expense of destroying other sanctuaries that until then had been considered legitimate in Judah. No doubt this carried a political cost with the cities that lost their sanctuaries, but this cost would not be great if we remember that Hezekiah did not control all of the Judahite territory, especially after Sennacherib's invasion in 701. The destruction of sanctuaries may have been a much greater issue on paper than in physical reality, and, if our hypothesis about the people of the land is correct, he had the support of the provincial elite for this measure, regardless.

From Hezekiah's reign comes an abundant literature—historical, wisdom, and prophetic. This is perfectly logical when we remember that this was a moment of reflection on the past, a moment for seeking the basis on which to construct a new future. It was probably in connection with the effort to make of Jerusalem the cultural and religious center of all Israel, including the Assyrian provinces to the north, that we are to understand the intense historical work.

It is at this time that we should place the combination of the Yahwist history of the origins (J) with the Elohist version of the same traditions (E). This combination is known in biblical studies as the Jehovist (JE). For the most part this combination simply incorporates elements of the northern Elohist version into the southern narration, which, in contrast, seems to have been preserved in its entirety in the new combined history. With this procedure, the redactors (R^{JE}) reflected the political realities of the moment, but there is a place within the narration of the origins of Israel where the redaction left its own stamp, in chapters 32 to 34 of Exodus. Here the story of the golden calf, originally a reflection on the Bethel sanctuary, has been used to separate the two gifts of the tables of the law, the Elohist (Exod. 20) and the Yahwist (Exod. 34). The intermediate texts, which are products of the court of Hezekiah, pose a theological reflection on sin (the making of the golden calf), punishment (the withdrawal of the divine present with Israel), and forgiveness leading to a new giving of the law. The same theological problem dominates the Jehovist redaction, which follows the sin of the people in not responding to the challenge of Caleb to enter the land that had been explored (Num. 14:11-13). From these two places where redactional activity is prominent it is evident that the elaboration of a new text JE served the purpose of underlining the possibility of forgiveness and a new beginning for Israel. This was a most relevant theological issue in the wake of the destruction of the kingdom of Israel.

It is also likely that the first version of the history of the Kings was written in the court of Hezekiah. If the analyses of Manfred Weippert are correct, this history would have begun its account with the reigns of Jotham of Israel (852–841 B.C.E.) and Jehoshaphat of Judah (873–848) in order to lead up to the capture of Samaria by the Assyrians and the theological reflection on the reasons for that catastrophe (2 Kings 17). Weippert rests his case on detailed studies of the evaluating formulas on the various reigns in the books of Kings, but should even these not be convincing it is natural to suppose that the abundance of material on the kingdom of Israel and the length and importance of the theological reflection on the fall of Samaria in our books of Kings came from Hezekiah's court shortly after these events that changed the political configuration of Palestine.

It was also at this time that we should place the historical work that presents the taking of Palestine by the tribes of Israel as a conquest carried out under the leadership of Joshua. We refer to the pre-Deuteronomistic collection of materials that are now in Joshua, chapters 1 to 11. Formerly, this collection was attributed to the Elohist of the Pentateuch, but there are no stylistic or theological reasons for this attribution. Martin Noth attributes it to a "compilator" whom he places around the year 900 B.C.E., but the period of the two kingdoms of Israel and Judah is a less likely context for the creation of a unified conquest story than the reign of Hezekiah, when there was a concerted effort to create a consciousness of national unity in the face of the loss of so much territory to the Assyrians. So, taking the ancient traditions, mainly from the Gilgal sanctuary plus some from Gibeon and Hazor, a vision was formed of the occupation of Palestine by the tribes as a single conquest under the blessing of Yahweh. One of the effects of this literary work, unfortunate from the viewpoint of the poor, was to displace from the national memory the class struggle that took place in Canaan at the time of the origins of Israel. Thus, in the Bible the Exodus no longer has a counterpart in the uprisings and migrations within the land of Canaan.

Other sorts of literary works were also composed at the court of Hezekiah. Collections of proverbs were made, which were attributed to Solomon (Prov. 25:1). This production was the work of Jerusalem functionaries who had an interest in maintaining a professional continuity in serious devotion to the daily work of the court rather than in looking for lessons in recent or ancient history.

Even outside the court this was a creative moment. The prophet Micah called on the peasants to arise and take possession of the land with the blessing of Yahweh (Mic. 2:1-5, 6-11). Micah not only did not share the official enthusiasm for the centralization of cultic life in Jerusalem, he called for the destruction of the city as the center of the bloody deeds committed against the people (Mic. 3:1-4, 9-12).

All we have seen up to now should be placed in the earlier part of Hezekiah's reign, before the invasion of Sennacherib (701). After the invasion survival was the main objective of all thinking persons in the kingdom. The life of Isaiah encompassed the whole of this period up through Sennacherib's invasion. During the reform and rereading of the past Isaiah took distance from these projects, asking above all for faith and confidence in Yahweh (Isa. 7:9; 14:24-27; 20:1-6). Like Micah, he saw too much evil in Jerusalem to expect that the projects of the capital would prove the salvation for the country (Isa. 1:21-26; 10:1-4), but he believed that Yahweh would see to it that Jerusalem would be purified to become again holy as at first (Isa. 1:21-26; 14:28-32). Isaiah's position in the face of the invasion of 701 is a hotly disputed issue. Perhaps he believed that, in spite of his reservations about the king's programs, in this crisis survival called for closing ranks and supporting Hezekiah, as it is claimed for him (2 Kings 19:1-7, 20-34).

If we follow Simon de Vries's reconstruction of the chronology, as we have done systematically in this book, Manasseh began to reign alongside his father Hezekiah in 697, four years after the invasion and dismembering of Judah. Later memories, both in 2 Kings and in 2 Chronicles, underscore a radical rupture between the innovative policies of Hezekiah and the consistent submission to the empire by Manasseh. It is this posture that rates Manasseh the worst assessment of all the kings of Judah according to the Deuteronomic historians (2 Kings 21:1-18). His coregency from the tender age of twelve can be understood as an Assyrian imposition, accepted by Hezekiah as preferable to the incorporation of Judah as a province of the empire. With Manasseh the ambitious projects of making out of Jerusalem the cultural and religious center of a renewed Israel were filed away. The "high places" were again tolerated. Some local interests of Levites and others were no doubt satisfied, but the dream of a unified Israel was abandoned. Manasseh allowed the return of non-Yahwistic cults to the temple and the high places in the cities. For this reason he is roundly condemned by the Deuteronomists. It is possible, however, that these were the only measures possible if Judah was to avoid the fate of Israel. If we are to believe the report of 2 Chronicles (33:14-17, not reported in 2 Kings), during the last part of his long reign he restored the walls of Jerusalem and rebuilt the altar of Yahweh. Even if the conversion of Manasseh (2 Chron. 33:12-13) shows the peculiar theological interests of the Chronicler and is not reported in 2 Kings, it is not unlikely that with the decline of Assyrian power in his last years, he may have been able to recover lost territories that had been incorporated into the Philistine provinces and had attempted to restore the symbols of Judahite nationality.

It is likely that it was in the years that followed Sennacherib's invasion and the closing of the project of national renewal that those who had supported the project undertook to put in writing a version of the book of the law of Moses that would later have great importance in Judah. This book of Moses, which we know as Deuteronomy, was a revised version of the traditional oral (and written) law attributed to Moses, put into the form of a farewell speech delivered in the plains of Moab before the people crossed the Jordan River under the leadership of Joshua. It became the legal basis for the reform of Josiah in the late sixth century. Some of its important characteristics are listed here:

1. The exclusive place of Jerusalem for the worship of Yahweh, mentioned often in thinly veiled form as "the place that Yahweh shall choose to make his name reside there" (Deut. 12:1-14).

2. The establishment of a volunteer army and the restoration of the ancient rules of the "war of Yahweh" (Deut. 20:1-10; 21:10-14).

3. A view of the king as a humble servant of Yahweh who scrupulously follows Yahweh's law, turning aside from too many riches, too many women, and a strong army (Deut. 17:14-20).

4. Following the experience of Israel, the prophets received a strong role, with the real authority in national affairs (Deut. 18:9-22).

5. The vehement condemnation of any cult foreign to Yahweh (Deut. 13:2-19).

6. Several of the laws have the purpose of guaranteeing the Levites a decent living so that they not be left in misery as a result of the closing of the "high places" of Judah where they previously served as state functionaries (Deut. 18:1-8).

As a whole, it is clear that this legal revision was made under the influence of the political project of Hezekiah and with the strong influence of the refugees from Israel in Jerusalem. The book, the result of a lot of work on the traditions of Israel and Judah, was placed in the Temple to wait for the right moment, which came during the reign of Josiah (640–609).

10
The Project of a New Israel
640-609 B.C.E.

Toward the end of the seventh century B.C.E., when Assyrian power suffered weakening and then a total collapse, the leaders of Judahite society made a great effort to restore Israel to a condition similar to its ancient glory. In modern interpretation we know this effort as the reform of Josiah, by the name of the king who directed it (640–609 B.C.E.).

Josiah's policy of renewal was guided by the measures of the "book of the law," which was found in the Temple (2 Kings 22:8-10; 2 Chronicles 34:14-18). When one compares the measures that Josiah took with the dispositions of Deuteronomy it becomes clear that the book of the law was substantially our book of Deuteronomy. The similarities between many of the measures taken by Josiah and the program of Hezekiah almost a century earlier can be explained by the theory, which we support, that Deuteronomy was written after the failure of Hezekiah's reform. Deuteronomy codified the legal tradition of Israel in the light of Hezekiah's project in the hope that another opportunity would present itself to carry out what Sennacherib's invasion had frustrated. In fact the opportunity did present itself when Assyrian power withdrew from Palestine.

Josiah sought legitimacy for his throne and his program of reform in an alliance (covenant) among Yahweh, king, and people (2 Kings 23:1-3). This was interpreted as a renewal of the alliance Moses established between Yahweh and the people in Moab just before his death (Deut. 29:9-14), with the significant modification that the king now assumed the role of mediator and guarantor of the alliance.

The authors of Deuteronomy, in spite of their obvious antecedents in the prophetic movement that began with Samuel, admitted the legitimacy of kings in Israel, although their legislation concerning the kings is more concerned to limit royal power than simply to define it (Deut. 17:14-20). The project of renewal as it is posed in the book lacks a subject with the power to implement it. The refugees who wrote it saw with realism the need to give to Jerusalem and its Temple a monopoly so that it might become the center around which the nation would gather. It must have been a bitter concession for the northerners. Having conceded so much, they were not ready to give a "metaphysical" legitimacy to the king as the son of Yahweh in the manner of the Davidic theology. It seems that both Hezekiah and then Josiah saw the need to soften their propagandistic language so as not to offend the sensibilities of the Israelites, whose adherence was necessary if they aspired to become the leaders of the nation Israel (and not just Judah).

Still, the agent with the capacity of implementing the profound reforms demanded by the book of the Alliance, another name for Deuteronomy, could only be the king of Jerusalem. That is, by yielding somewhat in his theological rhetoric, the king won the support of the refugees and, with that support, the possibility of winning over the population of the Assyrian provinces of Dor, Meguiddo, Gilead, and Samaria. Josiah proceeded to destroy all the sanctuaries "from Geba to Beersheba" (2 Kings 23:8), but he failed to fulfill the law that stipulated that the Levites displaced by these measures were to have access to the Temple on the same level of authority and participation as the Zadokite priests (2 Kings 23:9, compare Deut. 18:6-8). We have to suppose that Josiah's problem was the resistance of the priests of the Temple, on whom he was already imposing new customs and traditions (Deuteronomic ones). They would not have accepted being displaced or seeing their authority curtailed in their own Temple.

Beginning in the eighth year of his reign (632 B.C.E.) Josiah penetrated into the territory of the provinces of Samaria, Meguiddo, and Philistia to destroy the places of worship to Yahweh and the pagan sanctuaries that the Israelite population supported in those provinces (2 Chron. 34:3-7). This would only have been possible if Assyrian pow-

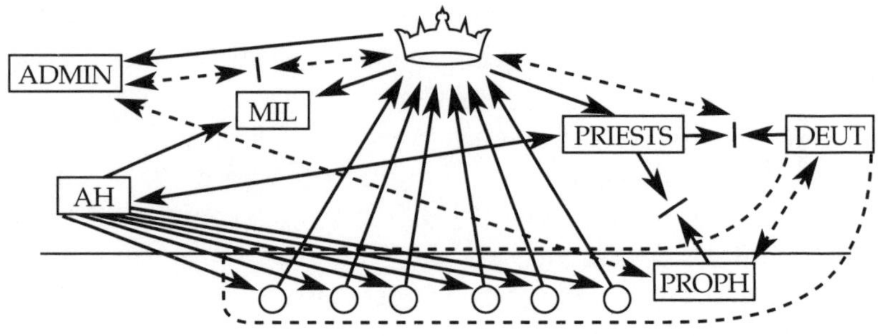

Diagram 11

er was already in a state of decay. The climactic moment was the destruction of the sanctuary of Bethel, once the main sanctuary of Israel (2 Kings 23:15), an act that was probably carried out only late in the reform, as is indicated by the location of the description of its destruction in the text. The completion of this great Israelite renewal in the eighteenth year of his reign (622 B.C.E.) was celebrated with a great Passover feast in the city of Jerusalem (2 Kings 23:21-23).

What did all this activity mean for the base of society, the poor people of Israel (including Judah)? We shall try to answer this crucial question with the help of diagram 11, above. Much in this diagram is familiar. At the base are the peasant villages, the productive units of society, with little relation among themselves. The Deuteronomic project and its implementation by Josiah did not include the renewal of tribal life. At the peak of society was the king, who extracted tribute from the produce of the land

and the services of the villages (the arrows from the villages to the king in diagram 11). The three bureaucratic apparatuses with which we are familiar, administrative (ADMIN), military (MIL), and priestly (PRIESTS) depend on the king. Now we move on to examine the new elements in this scheme.

The point of departure for understanding the political correlation within the ruling class is the assassination of Amon, Josiah's father, in the year 640 B.C.E.

> The servants of Amon conspired against him and killed the king in his house. The people of the land killed all those who conspired against King Amon and the people of the land proclaimed his son Josiah king in his stead (2 Kings 21:23-24).

The *'am ha'aretz*, "people of the land" (AH in the diagram), are not new actors on the national scene. It was they who, together with the Temple personnel, conspired to kill the queen Athaliah in 835 and to restore the Davidic dynasty with the youthful Joash (2 Kings 11:1-20). The "people of Judah" put Uzziah (Azariah) on the throne after the murder of Amaziah in a Jerusalem conspiracy (2 Kings 14:19-21), probably this same social group. It does not seem bold to suggest that this sector had interests in common with the Davidic king and with the priestly personnel that was the ideological support of the dynasty.

The conspiracies usually came, according to a repeated pattern, from the "servants of the king." This designation applies to the whole apparatus of state. Within that apparatus, the priests had a special interest, a theological interest, in supporting the Davidic dynasty. If indeed it is possible that they were responsible for the murder of Joash, it was because of a conjunctural dispute and did not have the intention of removing the dynasty (2 Kings 12:21-22, cf. 2 Chron. 24:27-22). Their loyalty to the Davidic line was unconditional.

We may suppose, on the other hand, that if the army had at some time been implicated in a royal assassination, it would not have been possible for the people of the land to frustrate their plans without a struggle, which would have left traces in the literature. By simple elimination we are left with the administrators as the sector of the servants of the king that could produce royal murderers. It is easy to see that this sector lacked a political base to impose its candidates for kings on society. As a result the assassinations proved fruitless. Their potential for conflict with the king is indicated in diagram 11 by arrows on broken lines, broken because the occasional opposition was not able to break the permanent dependence on the king in which they lived.

Who were the *'am ha'aretz*? We can hardly think of the peasant villages, which did not have sufficient organization to be able to function as agents in the struggles in Jerusalem. A striking but, unfortunately, not unambiguous statement in Jeremiah indicates that the people of the land may have been responsible for the recruitment of the soldiers for the army (Jer. 52:25). If this were a stable function of this sector it would give it an obvious importance for the king. This appears as the solid arrow from AH to MIL in diagram 11. The contrast with the inhabitants of the city (suggested by 2 Kings 11:20), which we saw previously, makes it probable that the people of the land were provincial landholders, the same who were denounced by Micah (Mic. 2:1-5) and Isaiah (Isa. 5:8-10). We are to understand, therefore, that the Judahite countryside was controlled by a limited number of landholders, and that these enjoyed close relations with the king (the Davidic kings), the army, and the Jerusalem priesthood. The peasants depended on them for their subsistence, that is, for the land with which to work, which allowed them to control the supply of young men for the army. This combination of relations is indicated by the solid arrows in the diagram.

A fourth block, the Deuteronomic group (DEUT) appears in the diagram at the same level as the state apparatuses. According to a theory, which we have accepted, this sector was made up of refugees from the north with cultural knowledge, that is, intellectuals. Under the influence of Hezekiah and Josiah they reformulated the ancient traditions of Israel in the hope that from Jerusalem it would be possible to breathe new life into the people of Yahweh. Their project was formulated as a "covenant," an agreement between Yahweh, the God of the Exodus, and Israel, the people of Yahweh. Moses the prophet was the mediator of the covenant which, according to the northern traditions, had been established at first at Mount Sinai and then renewed under the direction of the same Moses on the plains of Moab. In each successive generation Yahweh would lead the people by means of new prophets "like Moses" (Deut. 18:14-22), among whom prophets like Ahijah, Elijah, Elisha, Amos, and Hosea were remembered. According to this view of the alliance, the king played a limited role, a role limited by the law of Yahweh and by the word of Yahweh issued by means of God's servants, the prophets. The authority of these prophets could even extend to the removal of kings with whom they supposed Yahweh was displeased, as happened by means of Samuel, Ahijah, Jehu son of Hanani, and Elisha. The Deuteronomic group did not recognize in their law book any privilege to the Davidides. Their concession to them was the tacit recognition of Jerusalem as the sole legitimate place of worship, put in writing in the law (Deut. 12:1-14). This positive but reluctant relationship with the Judahite kings is represented in diagram 11 by a broken arrow.

The Deuteronomic project was an alternative to the project favored by the Jerusalem priesthood, a fact that is indicated in the diagram by opposing arrows. In the generation that followed Josiah this opposition appeared in two different historical works, the so-called Deuteronomistic history (Dtr = Deuteronomy + Joshua + Judges + Samuel + Kings) and the priestly version of the founding of Israel, which is woven into our present Pentateuch (the "P" source).

We must only establish the role of the prophets in Judah (PROPH in diagram 11). Properly speaking, this is not a social block like the previous ones. Prophets were individuals who claimed inspiration from Yahweh, the God of Israel, in order to announce God's word and to defend the poor. We know of five prophets during the period of Assyrian domination and the reform who played this role, three of whom were remembered as enemies of the Temple. The five were Isaiah, Micah, whose call for a peasant revolution we have noted, Zephaniah, Uriah (see Jer. 26:20-23), and Jeremiah.

Zephaniah during the reign of Josiah denounced the luxury and crimes of the dominant classes (Zeph. 1:8-9, 12-13; 3:1-4). Zephaniah opposed the powerful on "my holy hill" with the poor and humble people, "the lowly of the land" (*'anwe ha'aretz*), who would find protection on the day of the wrath of Yahweh (Zeph. 2:1-3; 3:11-13). In these expressions we have an opposition to the state and its religious apparatus, and yet the prophet makes no mention of the Deuteronomic reformers and their project of a new covenant. Although Zephaniah does not call for revolution, his is without a doubt a people's position in opposition to the leaders of his time.

Concerning Uriah we know only that he was a martyr because of his accusations against the Temple in the name of Yahweh. This did not happen until the days of Jehoiachim (609–598). We only mention him in this context because he is a witness to the presence of a native Judahite Yahwistic tradition contrary to the Temple.

We are better informed concerning Jeremiah. Jeremiah came from a priestly family of Anathoth of Benjamin. His confrontation with the Temple is preserved in an eloquent sermon (Jer. 7:1-15). This is not surprising in the light of the same position held by Micah and Uriah, and of what seems an implicit condemnation of the Temple in Zephaniah. More surprising is the fact that Jeremiah condemns Josiah's reform as "false" (Jer. 3:6-13). Samaria, says Jeremiah, was more honest than Jerusalem, because Samaria never pretended to have converted. The conversion of Jerusalem was a dishonest conversion, because injustice continued to be the basis of national life except for thinking Yahweh was on Jerusalem's side. They have turned the Temple called by Yahweh's name into a den of thieves! (Jer. 7:11).

These prophets, then, take up the people's cause against their oppressors, which include kings, priests, scribes, and even Deuteronomic reformers. Jeremiah later made a pact with a sector of the administrative bureaucracy. The book that draws his prophecies together shows a strong Deuteronomistic influence in its style, indicating that at least some Deuteronomists saw him and his writings as an ally in their later ideological struggles with the priestly caste. These poorly defined relations are indicated by the broken line in diagram 11.

The reform directed by King Josiah came to an abrupt end with his violent death at the hands of the king of Egypt in 609 when he was only 39 years old. Nevertheless, through the writing of the Deuteronomists, the reform left a permanent mark on the life of Israel. The work of the Maccabees/Hasmoneans five centuries later can be seen as a revival of the project of Josiah, about which we shall see more later.

11
The Babylonian Hegemony 605-539 B.C.E.

The Political History

The great experiment in national renewal that was guided by the book of Deuteronomy ended abruptly with the death of Josiah at the hands of the king of Egypt in 609 B.C.E. (2 Kings 23:29-30). During four years Egypt imposed a tribute on the land (one hundred talents of silver and one of gold), over which it had put as king Jehoiachim, one of the sons of Josiah (2 Kings 23:33-35). It seems likely that his authority included those parts of the province of Samaria that Josiah had subjected to his authority.

In 605 the two powers that aspired to take control over what had been Assyrian-dominated territories fought. Babylon was able to defeat the Egyptian army in a battle fought at Carchemish. Jeremiah reflected on this event (Jeremiah 46). As a result, Babylon became the new hegemonic power in Palestine. Jehoiachim began to pay tribute to Babylon but was able to stay on as king of Judah. Nonetheless, the old provincial system imposed by Assyria was restored and Samaria was again separated from Judah.

Shortly before his death in 598 Jehoiachim started to retain his tribute. A punitive expedition from Babylon reached Jerusalem early in 597 when his son Jehoiachin had been on the throne barely three months. Apparently as a punishment (and not as a permanent measure of population redistribution) Nebuchadnezzar took the king and several members of the royal family, plus metalworkers and locksmiths and other persons of social value to Babylon, in total 3,023 persons (Jer. 52:28; 2 Kings 24:14 says they were 10,000, a round number, which is less likely to be accurate). Over the vassal kingdom of Judah the Babylonians left Zedekiah, an uncle of the king and son of Josiah (2 Kings 24:17). The political result was a division of loyalties in Judah: Part of the population recognized Zedekiah and another part continued to hope for the return of Jehoiachin, whom they considered the legitimate king. (This situation underlies Jeremiah's vision of the baskets of figs, one good and one bad, in Jeremiah 24.)

Zedekiah developed ambitions to make Palestine independent under the leadership of Judah. In order to plan this he called to Jerusalem the representatives of the kings of various peoples subject to Babylon: Edom, Moab, Ammon, Tyre, and Sidon (Jer. 27:2-3). The result was disastrous. Nebuchadnezzar brought a military expedition, besieged Jerusalem, and took it in 586, the ninth day of the month of Tammuz (2 Kings 25:1-5). Seeing the need to finish once and for all with Judahite dreams of grandeur, the Babylonians destroyed their strong fort, Jerusalem. The walls and the Temple were brought to the ground and the city was burned down so that it could no longer serve for human habitation. To administer the territory they named a certain Gedaliah, a government functionary who had no ties of kinship with the Davidic family line (2 Kings 25:22-26; Jeremiah 40–41). He made his administrative center the city of Mizpah, just a little north of Jerusalem, and restored some normalcy (Jer. 40:11-12).

Some of the rulers of Judah had sought refuge with the king of Ammon, and from Ammon they conspired to restore an independent Judah, probably an unrealistic dream given the circumstances of the moment. The prophet Jeremiah, who serves as a barometer to measure the people's interests at this difficult moment, threw his lot with Gedaliah (Jer. 40:6). The nation was, then, divided into at least three parts in their political loyalties: (1) those who supported the government of Gedaliah, which had the protection of Babylon; (2) the exiles in Babylon who continued to place their hopes in King Jehoiachin who was confined in Babylon (They apparently also had some support in Judah.); (3) the group that had taken refuge in Ammon, concerning whose political projects we are not informed.

A certain Ishmael emerged from this last group. With a group of supporters he murdered Gedaliah and the bodyguard of Babylonian soldiers who defended him in Mizpah (Jer. 41:1-3). This happened in the seventh month of an undetermined year (2 Kings 25:25-26). Because it should probably be tied to the deportation of 745 persons to Babylon in the year 582 (Jer. 52:30), this would mean that Gedaliah's government lasted just under four years. His team of government in Mizpah left for a voluntary exile in Egypt, taking the prophet Jeremiah with them by force (Jeremiah 42).

Judah was left completely demoralized and disorganized. A total of 4,600 persons were deported to Babylon on three different occasions, in 597, 586, and 582 (Jer. 52:27-30). There they were confined under a strictly local freedom. Others fled to Egypt, Ammon, and other nations. The humble peasant people remained in their places working the land. After the assassination of Gedaliah Judah was annexed to the province of Samaria. The Babylonians never gave a definitive resolution to a new population that they might have brought to govern the country.

The Babylonian Empire was shaken at its core by the emergence of a Persian king who was able to put together in a powerful empire the forces of Media and Persia. This Cyrus came to power in 550 B.C.E. and already in the winter of 547–546 he carried out a spectacular campaign in Asia Minor where he defeated the legendary King Creossus of Lydia. Babylonia was on the defensive, but Cyrus did nothing against it until 539. By that year the internal decomposition had advanced to such a degree that the Babylonians themselves opened the gates of the city to the approaching Cyrus, who was able to enter without besieging or damaging the city. From the perspective of the history of Israel this ended a Babylonian period that was little more than an interlude between the Assyrian and the Persian empires, both of which had more lasting consequences for the configuration of Israel.

The Political Stance of the Prophet Jeremiah

Any effort to read the events of this period from the viewpoint of the poor must rest largely on the political activity of Jeremiah who during his long career adopted a dissident position with respect to the policies of the kings.

Jeremiah came from Anathoth, a Levitical city within the territory that was traditionally assigned to the tribe of Benjamin. He was born into a priestly family, probably the family of the Levitical priest Abiathar who was deported by Solomon to Anathoth in the tenth century (1 Kings 2:26-27). In his attacks against the Temple of Jerusalem (Jer. 7:1—8:3; 26:1-24) he was part of a prophetic lineage that went back to Micah of Moreshet-Gath (Mic. 3:9-12) and included his contemporary Uriah of Kiriath-Jearim (Jer. 26:20-23). In spite of his affinity with the northern prophets whose influence is prominent in Deuteronomy, he kept his distance from the Josianic reform (Jer. 3:6-13). All of this leads us to believe that a native religious movement that never supported the Davidic theology of the Temple existed in Judah. The influx of northerners after the fall of Samaria in 722 B.C.E. would have strengthened this sector, which would have been closer to the people than to the priests in the Temple.

During the reign of Zedekiah (597–586) Jeremiah consistently supported a policy of subjection to Babylon, and for that reason he condemned the king's policies built on alliances with other nations (Jeremiah 27). Nebuchadnezzar, the king of Babylon, was the "servant of Yahweh" (minister of Yahweh) to afflict Judah and Jerusalem because they had not listened to the voice of Yahweh's messengers the prophets (Jer. 25:1-12). This conviction went so far that, during the siege of the city of Jerusalem, Jeremiah advised the soldiers to lay down their arms and turn themselves over to the Babylonians who surrounded the city (Jer. 21:1-10). For this treasonous preaching he was imprisoned by the king and the other authorities (Jer. 37:11-12). He was also the object of a murder plot by a group of men from

Anathoth (Jer. 11:21), although, unfortunately, we do not know when this happened. That incident should probably be put early in his career, during the life of Josiah, at a moment when we suppose that a majority of the men of Anathoth supported the king's reforms, which Jeremiah opposed.

The exiled community in Babylon hoped for the restoration of Jehoiachin on David's throne. Jeremiah disappointed them. He urged them to cast down roots in that land from which they would not return until seventy years had passed; that is, only their children or grandchildren might hope to return (Jeremiah 29). This does not mean that Jeremiah favored the group that stayed in Jerusalem and supported Zedekiah. On the contrary, between these two groups Jeremiah saw a greater future for the former, whom he compares to a good basket of figs in comparison to which the other groups was a basket of spoiled figs (Jeremiah 24).

What, then, was Jeremiah's political stance? We can derive the first clue from his action of leaving the besieged city to buy a piece of property in Anathoth (Jeremiah 32). In so doing the prophet announced the proximate return to a normal life in which it would be possible to plant and harvest the fields. His idea about how this would come about is tied to the political project of Gedaliah (a court functionary who was a grandson of Shaphan, a scribe in Josiah's government), to whom the Babylonians had commissioned the organization of national life under their protection (Jeremiah 40). Jeremiah saw the salvation of the people in a distancing from the house of David and the priesthood of Jerusalem to seek life under the protection of Babylon. More than twenty-five centuries later it is hard for us to challenge Jeremiah's analysis of what was best for the people of Judah, although it is hard to believe that in the long run such a project could be responsive to the people's needs. A sovereign state with a solid base in the popular classes would be necessary for the long run, but we can accept the analysis of Jeremiah for the short run as the way to free the people from a Davidic rule that could not satisfy its needs.

The Literature of the Babylonian Period

This was a period rich in history writing. The same circle that produced the legal revision that we call Deuteronomy also made a magnificent reading of the history of Israel called by modern exegetes the Deuteronomistic History (Dtr). Taking for its theological bearings the Deuteronomic Law and the Josianic reform, the history was read since Moses, going through the conquest of Canaan, the struggles of the judges, the establishment of the monarchy, the division of the kingdoms, the fall of Samaria, and culminating in the reform.

A first edition of this work (Dtr^1) was written after the reform and before the destruction of Jerusalem. It told how Moses had put before the people on the plains of Moab the laws that Yahweh had given on Sinai for their life in the land of Canaan. During their long history Yahweh had sent them prophets to bring God's Word up to date, but during the time of the judges the tribes insisted on abandoning Yahweh for other gods. Yahweh turned them over to their enemies, but when they cried out in anguish Yahweh raised a liberator for them (Judg. 2:6-19). Yahweh gave them kings to lead them better, but they insistently followed the sinful path with which Jeroboam had misled them and Yahweh finally gave them over to the Assyrians (2 Kings 17:7-41). Nevertheless, foreseeing this type of problem, Yahweh had established a Temple in Jerusalem as a place of prayer (not so much of sacrifices!) so that the repentant people could ask forgiveness (1 Kings 8:14-61). This is precisely what the people did under the guidance of good King Josiah (2 Kings 22:11; 23:1-3). If they persevered in their faithfulness, Yahweh would fulfill to them all the blessings which had been promised through Moses (Deut. 28:1-4).

The destruction of the Temple was a harsh blow to the historical faith (faith in the history as it was remembered as a history of salvation) of the Deuteronomists. When some years had passed, around 561 B.C.E. (see 2 Kings

25:27), these circles made a modification of their history, a revision that exegetes today know as Dtr^2. This revision of Dtr underscored the law as the only basis for the life of Israel and also underscored the constant rebellion of Israel (and to a lesser extent Judah). The monarchy itself is viewed as rebellion (1 Sam. 8:7; 12:19). The story was completed with the sad events of the kings who were the sons of Josiah (2 Kings 24, 25). What we have in the Bible today is this revised version of Dtr in the books of Deuteronomy, Joshua, Judges, Samuel, and Kings.

The Deuteronomists were not the only ones to propose to Israel a project of national salvation supported by a reading of their history with Yahweh. If we follow the arguments of Richard Elliott Friedman, which seem convincing, it was during this dramatic period that we should place the revisionist reading of the origins of Israel that we know as the priestly stratum of the Pentateuch (P).

In the court of Hezekiah and under pre-Deuteronomic influences the two older versions, the Judahite version (J) and the Israelite version (E) of the origins of Israel had been combined into one. The result was the history we know as Jehovist (JE). From the viewpoint of the Jerusalem priests this history had some serious defects. Let us mention a few:

1. The patriarchs offered sacrifices in an uncontrolled manner, without having received from Yahweh the revelation about how, when, and by whom sacrifices should be done correctly. In their alternative version (P), Abraham, Isaac, and Jacob never make sacrifices (nor do Cain, Abel, or Noah).

2. The history of the golden calf in which Aaron, the father of the priests, appears as the prime culprit (Exodus 32), was unacceptable. Besides, in this history the Levites were exalted for killing the apostates, and Aaron was saved only because of his status as the brother of Moses (Exod. 32:25-29). In their version this incident disappeared from the story and two stories

are added, which exalt Aaron and his descendents, that is, the story of the rebellion of Korah, son of Kohath, the son of Levi, and the heavenly support for Aaron (Numbers 16–17), and the story about the "zeal" of Pinechas in the face of the apostasy at Peor (Num. 25:6-18).

3. Joshua, the successor of Moses and an Ephraimite, appeared in JE as the companion of Moses in the censored history of the golden calf (Exod. 32:17) and, what was worse, he was always in the tent of meeting (Exod. 33:11), something forbidden to one who was not a priest or even a Levite. So P eliminates these references to Joshua, and instead exalts the virtues of the successor of Moses by making him a companion of Caleb in the exploration of the land of Canaan (Numbers 13).

With these three elements, we can see the tendency of this priestly work, which intended to displace JE, by telling the same story from a perspective more acceptable to the Jerusalem priests.

The project of the priests can be understood from the importance of the Tabernacle as the axis of the revelation of Yahweh on Mount Sinai (Exod. 25:8-9). Maintaining the sacrifices on the altar, which was to be placed in front of the Tabernacle, would guarantee to Israel the presence of Yahweh. The Deuteronomistic traditions recognized (1 Kings 8:4) what the priests would later underline in their version of the history (2 Chron. 5:4; 1:1-6), that the Tabernacle during the monarchy was placed within the Jerusalem Temple. The effect of this placement was that the priests, like the Deuteronomists, insisted on the monopoly of the Temple of Solomon. For them the monopoly was based on the fact that the altar before the Tabernacle was the only legitimate place to offer the sacrifices Yahweh demanded of the people. The fundamental law in this sense is found at the very beginning of the "holiness code" (Lev. 17:1-7).

The rivalry between these two projects finds its center of conflict in their respective ruling concerning the "Levites" who were not descendents of Aaron. According to the law (Deut. 18:1-8) all Levites may be able to claim all the rights of any other priest only by presenting themselves in the place that Yahweh shall choose. According to P, however, the Levites could only exercise minor functions, while the role of offering sacrifices upon the altar before the Tabernacle was reserved exclusively for the sons of Aaron (Exod. 29:1-30; Leviticus 8–9). The measures adopted by Josiah in his reform were a middle ground (2 Kings 23:9), because the Levites were not admitted to the service of the altar but did receive a portion from the altar for their subsistence.

The Uncertainty Concerning the Reform

We have seen that in this period there was a coexistence of at least three projects that claimed a support in the traditions of the God Yahweh. The dominant project, because of the powerful support it drew from Josiah, was the Deuteronomist project, and it was this reading of the history of Israel that established itself. Alongside it the project of the priests of the Temple continued to exist, a project that shared with the former one an emphasis on the monopoly of Jerusalem seen, not as the residence for the name of Yahweh as for the Deuteronomists, but as the residence for Yahweh, pure and simple (Deut. 12:5 vs. Exod. 25:8). Jeremiah and other prophets represented a people's version of the religious traditions of Israel that never accepted the monopoly of Jerusalem in either of its variant forms.

The destruction of Jerusalem with its Temple in 586 B.C.E. required a theological interpretation and received several. There is evidence of a popular religion that saw in the ritual purification undertaken by Josiah the cause for the ills that had fallen on Jerusalem (Jer. 44:15-19). By interrupting the rites addressed to the queen of heaven

Judah had provoked the disgrace. It was not, as the Deuteronomists claimed, a punishment for not having maintained the reform in its purity after the death of Josiah, but rather a punishment for having violated the cult place of Asherah, the queen of heaven.

We also know of the existence of an Israelite colony in Elephantine, an island on the upper Nile. There the Israelites had built a temple for Yahweh (and his consort!) without any feeling that this violated a divine command. These Israelites wrote in all innocence to the leaders of Jerusalem and Samaria to ask for guidance (in the late fifth century). This surprising bit of chance evidence shows that the reform with its demands of exclusiveness for Jerusalem was not able to impose itself in every place where Yahweh was worshiped in the Babylonian period. It is natural to suppose that some of the sanctuaries profaned by Josiah, like Bethel and Gilgal, were later restored.

On the other hand, Lamentations, attributed (incorrectly) to Jeremiah, is evidence for the existence in Judah of an interpretation of the destruction as the result of disobedience accompanied by a longing for the reconstruction of the Temple. This is an expression of poor people who remained in the land after the deportations ordered by Nebuchadnezzar! This, in addition to what we are told of the pilgrimages of those who went to the site of the Temple ruins to offer prayers and offerings (Jer. 41:5), permits the conclusion that the reform made a deep impression even on the peasants of the northern provinces. The Temple ruins became the location of lamentation rites in which the inhabitants of the land offered prayers like those gathered in Lamentations.

We may suppose, then, among the Israelites who remained in the now Babylonian provinces of Palestine, a situation that was religiously variegated and somewhat disordered, with a number of different positions represented. We have no information about the economic conditions of the peasants under their Babylonian governors. Politically, the provinces retained the lines of the Assyrian system except that Judah was incorporated into the province of Samaria after the murder of Gedaliah.

The Utopias of the Babylonian Exile Community

Meanwhile, the Israelite colony that lived in Babylon did not cease to dream of their return to Jerusalem. The nostalgia they felt is well expressed in the sad song of Psalm 137. The exiles were the elite of Jerusalem. Many of them put down roots in Babylon and their families never returned to Palestine, making Babylon an important center of Judaism for the future centuries. Among them were priests and Levites who had experience with the traditions of Israel. It is probable that Dtr^2 itself was carried out in Babylon, in light of the ending given to this revision with the release of Jehoiachin from confinement in that city. It was also here that two alternative visions of the restoration arose, each based on the preaching of a prophet, Ezekiel and Deutero-Isaiah (Isaiah 40–55), respectively.

Within Ezekiel there is a complete program for the restoration of Israel around a rebuilt Temple (Ezekiel 40–48). It is a variant of the vision of the Jerusalem priests, which we find in P. The whole geographical organization of the new Israel, the twelve reconstituted tribes, is arranged so as to protect the purity of the Temple, because it is believed that the disaster that overtook Jerusalem was the result of the impurities that contaminated the land of Yahweh (Ezek. 36:16-18). The access to the Temple would be zealously protected in the new Israel, and only the Zadokite priests would have authority in the Temple. The Levites would henceforth be excluded from the service of the altar because they had participated in the contamination of the holy objects (Ezek. 44:10-14). Once the Temple and its service was restored, a miraculous fountain would spring up beneath the altar and its waters would irrigate the land, which would produce in abundance along the path of the waters until it reached the Dead Sea, whose waters would be healed henceforth (Ezek.47:1-12).

The other utopian vision from the exiled community was formulated by an anonymous prophet whose sayings have been placed in Isaiah, chapters 40 to 55. Modern Bible students call him Deutero-Isaiah or the second Isaiah. This prophet is concerned to wipe out the guilt complex of the community, which he says has paid double for the fathers' sins (Isa. 40:1-2). For that reason the tone of his preaching is quite different from that of his prophetic predecessors. He does not practice denunciation against a people whose problem is not arrogance but discouragement. His is a call to confidence, in Yahweh and in themselves (see, for instance, Isa. 40:28-31). Yahweh is the Lord of history and it is God who has raised the great Persian King Cyrus, whose feats are astounding the world (Isa. 41:1-5; 45:1-7). These references to Cyrus make us suppose that the second Isaiah prophesied after Cyrus' campaign against Lydia (547 B.C.E.) and before he took Babylon (539).

Yahweh has the intention, according to the second Isaiah, of restoring Israel to its land, and for this he will prepare a highway in the desert making rivers and trees spring up (Isa. 40:3-11; 43:16-21). Jerusalem will rejoice in its restoration (Isa. 52:1-6; 51:1-3). Although he anticipates the rebuilding of the Temple, this is only part of the reconstruction of the city and receives only a passing mention, just once in the whole collection of prophecies (Isa. 44:28). The eternal promises to David will be fulfilled, not with a new king but with the paradise-like conditions of the whole people (Isa. 55:1-3). The people of Israel have a mission to fulfill among the nations of the earth (Isa. 49:6), because they must teach justice to the confines of the earth (Isa. 42:1-4). Even their sufferings have a saving value, because the nations will see and be astounded and believe when the servant, after suffering many indignities, is exalted by Yahweh (Isa. 52:13—53:12).

The messianic hopes announced by Isaiah in beautiful texts (like Isa. 9:1-6 and 11:1-9) are now to be fulfilled in Cyrus! Yahweh has taken Cyrus by the hand and given into his hands all the nations of the earth, even though Cyrus does not yet know God (Isa. 45:1-7). It is he who will carry out the return of the exiles and the rebuilding of Jerusalem and the Temple (Isa. 44:28).

It is difficult to situate this utopia among the social forces that we have seen up to now. It is not Deuteronomistic, for the characteristic themes of this current are not present. Much less is it priestly, as even a superficial comparison with Ezekiel will show. Mysteriously, it looks like a people's vision emerging among the elite exile community—except for one thing, the omission of any reference to the peasant community who made up the majority of the nation and for whom the exile was not a real factor. Thus it looks like a well-meaning effort to construct an honest and just project which, nevertheless, suffers from the inability of a member of the elite, in his dreams for the good society, to incorporate the toiling masses who feed us all. Still, the existence of this magnificent text had a significant influence on restored Judah under Persian hegemony.

12
The Persian Rule 539-332 B.C.E.

Cyrus entered the city of Babylon in 539 B.C.E. There he encountered, among others, the community of the descendents of the people who were taken captive from Jerusalem by Nebuchadnezzar. During the first year of his government in Babylon, surely in response to a petition from the exiles, he issued an edict returning the utensils of the Temple of Jerusalem to the people of Judah, represented by the person of Sheshbazzar (or Sanabassaros, according to the form the name receives in 1 Esdras 2:8). The edict (preserved in Ezra 1:2-4) authorizes the rebuilding of the Temple of Jerusalem and instructs the local authorities, who would be the rulers of the province of Samaria, to offer material assistance to that effect.

How should this edict be understood? By means of the Cyrus cylinder, discovered by archaeologists in Mesopotamia, it is known that Cyrus assumed the patronage of the Marduk cultus in Babylon. The inscription on the cylinder says that it was Marduk who pronounced his name so that he might be Lord Cyrus of the whole world. In light of this contemporary monumental inscription, it is not improbable that the emperor should have adopted a similar posture with respect to "Yahweh the God of heaven." The second Isaiah had already announced that Yahweh took Cyrus by the hand to give over to him the nations (Isa. 45:1), and certainly the king could accept this prophetic affirmation. Thereby he became a devotee of Yahweh and the patron of the Yahweh cult in Jerusalem. By underwriting the local cult he hoped to attain a degree of consensus for his administration, at least among the priests.

Who was this Sheshbazzar whom Ezra calls a "prince (*nasi'*) of Judah" (Ezra 1:8)? The key is probably in the form of his name in the apocryphal book of 1 Esdras, that is, Sanabassaros. In this form it looks like the same name as Shenazzar, which appears in the genealogy of 1 Chronicles as a son of Jehoiachin the Davidic king who died in exile (1 Chron. 3:17-24). The Persians, of course, were not restoring him to the throne of his father. His was the limited mission of returning the utensils of the Temple and undertaking the reconstruction. Of these tasks he was only able to carry out the first. The sources do not report his end. During the time of his mission he was not completely on his own, for Jerusalem was part of the province of Samaria, and the political supervision of the rebuilding of the Temple would be in the hand of the governor of that province. It seems that Sheshbazzar was able to begin the reconstruction but not to conclude it (that is the probable meaning of Ezra 4:24).

In the second year of Darius (520 B.C.E.), the rebuilding was begun anew under the direction of a new commissar named Zerubbabel, who was also from the family of David, the son of Shealtiel and grandson of Jehoiachin (Ezra 3:2 or, according to 1 Chron. 3:19, the son of Pedaiah and grandson of Jehoiachin; in either case, a Davidide). Once again, we must accept that his mission from the imperial authorities was specific and limited, with an authority and a temporal extension that were specific and under the control of the governor of Samaria.

A conflict emerged around the project (Ezra 4:1-5). The elite of the province who, one hundred years after Josiah had destroyed Bethel, had their own new Yahweh sanctuaries, saw the reconstruction of the famous Temple within their province as a threat. If the correspondence with Rehum the governor and Shimshai the secretary (Ezra 4:8-23) is authentic, there was a problem of administrative lack of communication, which probably ought to be located in the times of Cyrus or his successor Cyaxares (and not

Xerxes, as stated in Ezra 4:6). Once again there were problems with the project of Zerubbabel, about which the governor at Samaria had not been officially informed, but this time they were resolved by means of letters to and from the central offices of Darius (Ezra 5:6—6:18).

Besides the administrative confusion that was resolved through bureaucratic channels, a more serious problem arose of conflict with the "people of the land" (Ezra 4:4). If this means the same sector we know, the landholders of the rural areas, we can well understand their desire to participate in the Temple. During the times of the monarchy they had been loyal supporters of the kings and of the Temple built by Solomon, but now things had changed. The new Temple was being built by returned exiles. Remembering the settlement of strangers by the Assyrian King Esarhaddon, the exiles questioned the religious legitimacy of those who had stayed in Palestine. This type of conflict between those who experienced the exile and now returned with the support of the Persian government and those who had never left the land explains the great interest shown by the texts of this period in racial purity and family credentials. The genealogies were weapons that the exiles used against the Israelites of the land.

At the ideological level, this conflict of power can be seen clearly in the prophecies of this period. On the side of the exiles (the *Gola*, according to the Hebrew terminology) are situated the prophets Haggai and Zechariah who supported the rebuilding of the Temple with their words. On the opposite side, that of the people who were being excluded from sharing in the project, are situated the anonymous prophets whose sayings were gathered in Isaiah, chapters 56 to 66, which are called collectively the third Isaiah.

Let us look first at the prophets who spoke for the people. The most dramatic oracle (Isa. 66:1-2) denies that Yahweh has any interest in the Temple that the *Gola* is building because Yahweh made all things and needs nothing. Another (Isa. 58:1-12) condemns the rites of fasts that were a significant part of the liturgical calendar of the priests who controlled the post-exilic Temple: Yahweh desires the fast that liberates the oppressed and feeds the hungry. By bowing their heads like reeds they will not get Yahweh's interest. Yahweh is a God who dwells on high and at the same time with those who are ground down and humiliated on the earth (Isa. 57:15).

Third Isaiah has a critical word in the prophecy concerning the enthusiasm for genealogies which heads up the collection (Isa. 56:1-7). Yahweh accepts even eunuchs who keep God's sabbaths and the covenant, and the foreigner has full entry into the community. In fact, the Temple shall be called a "house of prayer for all the peoples" (Isa. 56:7). In the magnificent utopian vision (Isa. 65:17-25) the Temple is not even mentioned; the center of hope is long life and abundant food.

The anonymity of this beautiful collection of sayings may be due to the need to conceal the identities of the prophets. The prophecies were preserved only by placing them within Isaiah under the umbrella of that great prophet of the past. In the land ideological power was exercised by the priests of the *Gola*. The similarities of style, vocabulary, and even theology suggest that these people's prophets from the time of Darius were disciples of the great prophet of the exile whom we know as the second Isaiah.

On the side of the *Gola*, the prophets Haggai and Zechariah put their weight behind the construction of the Temple. They took the severe economic limitations of the time to be the result of the small offerings and weak efforts put into this cause (Hag. 1:2-11; 2:15-19). Haggai saw in Zerubbabel, the commissar responsible before the empire for the work, a new David chosen by Yahweh as a signet ring to "destroy the power of the nations" (Hag. 2:20-23).

The messianism of Zechariah introduced into Jewish theology the duality that would continue for many centuries to be a characteristic of some of its currents. Zerubbabel the commissar and Joshua the high priest are "the two anointed ones who are standing alongside the Lord of the whole earth" (Zech. 4:14). They are the two olive trees who provide with oil the seven lamps that adorn the lampstand, which the prophet saw in prophetic visions (Zech. 4:1-4). In another vision the prophet saw how Satan attacked Joshua, but Yahweh protected him, a protection symbolized by the clean garments God gave him (Zech. 3:1-7).

The confrontation between the *Gola* and the people of the land, which is reflected in the acrimonious dispute surrounding the building of the Temple under the auspices of the Persian government and also in the disputes about racial purity, is to a great extent a class struggle. On the one side, there were peasants and former landholding families apparently impoverished by the disorganization of the Babylonian period, faced by an exilic community that was well organized around a priestly religious project and with the economic and political backing of the Persian authorities. We can represent the situation that prevailed from the building of the Temple until the mission of Nehemiah (520–445 B.C.E.) in the following manner:

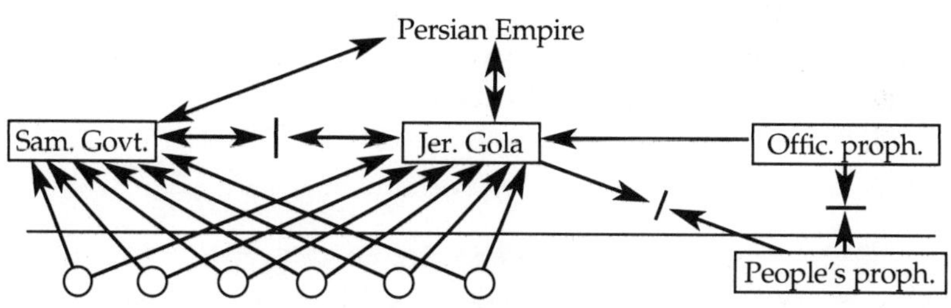

Diagram 12

In this diagram it is possible to appreciate that the relation of the villages, which continued to be the productive units in Israel, with the empire took place through a double mediation: first through the Persian governor of Samaria, and second through the Jerusalem priesthood, which had returned from the Babylonian exile and owed its position to the Persian authorities. The empire was initially disposed to pay for the establishment of the priestly caste although we may suppose that after the initial outlay the Temple became a net benefit for the empire. A difficulty with this system of domination was the inherent tension between the dominant elite of the province with its center in Samaria and the priesthood of Jerusalem. Each group had direct contacts with the Persian capitals of Ecbatana and Susa, but relations between them were not fluid and certainly not cordial.

The prophets of this period gathered in two opposed camps: On one side were the "official" prophets who served as an ideological support to the priestly caste; and on the other was a group of prophets whose names were not preserved because they clashed with the priests and the official prophets in the name of the popular interests. As far as the villages were concerned, including even the principal families (the "people of the land"), their relation with Samaria consisted of sending tribute, while their relation with the Jerusalem Temple and its priests was surely supportive, in general terms. In spite of some antagonistic interests articulated in the prophets' preaching, the Temple was after all the major expression of their cultic practice of the faith of Yahweh, the God of their fathers.

The Composition of the Pentateuch and the Mission of Ezra

When in the seventh year of Artaxerxes, Ezra "the scribe of the law of the God of heaven" was sent by the king on a mission to make the law known and effective among the inhabitants of Judah ("all those who in my reign belong to the people of Israel"), it is likely that what was happening was the proclamation of the Pentateuch. The edict is preserved in the original Aramaic (Ezra 7:13-26) in what may be its authentic form. If the Artaxerxes mentioned is the first king of that name, the year of Ezra's mission would have been 458 B.C.E. (Artaxerxes I governed from 465 to 424; the other possibility, less likely, is that the king was Artaxerxes II, who reigned from 404 to 358 B.C.E.)

The reading of the law by Ezra in a solemn assembly during seven days in Jerusalem (Neh. 8:1-18) brings to mind the proclamation of the book of the covenant, Deuteronomy, in the days of Josiah. This would have been, like that occasion, the official presentation of the law with the support of the civil authorities, in this case of the Persian province and the empire.

We can suppose then that the redaction of the Pentateuch was done during the first half of the fifth century B.C.E. The mere fact of its redaction reveals a unification that had taken place within the dominant class of Israelites. The work was done on the basis of two narratives about the origins of Israel, beginning in both cases with creation and ending with Moses. These narratives, JE and P, were antagonistic at several points. The combination of the Yahwist and Elohist narratives, as we have seen, was done under the auspices of the court of Hezekiah at the end of the eighth century. It placed much emphasis on the patriarchs, who even founded sanctuaries and sacrificed animals to Yahweh in places like Hebron and Bethel. It also exalted the figure of Moses, while it left a cloud of doubts over the integrity of Aaron. On the other hand, the priestly code (P) was a revisionist reading of the history, reducing the prominence of the patriarchs and exalting the figure of Aaron. It was only possible to combine these texts with such different points of view if the social forces which they each represented had reached a substantial degree of reconciliation.

In the redaction of the Pentateuch the first part of the Deuteronomistic History (Dtr) was also included, which dealt with the person of Moses. We have seen how during the last years of the reign of the Davidic dynasty there were tensions between the Deuteronomistic and the Priestly projects for the nation. The demise of the monarchy rendered irrelevant the main problems between these two groups of the Jerusalem elite.

The final outcome of the redaction of a single version of the origins of Israel, from the creation to the death of Moses, has a distinctly Priestly tone. Although it gathers up JE and Dtr, the general framework and the editorial comments give priority to the Priestly document (P) and its historical and theological viewpoints. This reflects the political realities of the strength of the priestly group that controlled the Temple and had the support of the empire. From a people's perspective, we would have to say that by the middle of the fifth century the dominant class had successfully achieved its unity.

The mission of Ezra, the implementation of the law of Moses, legitimated the dominant role of the Temple. Much of Moses' work at Sinai was to receive the model of the Tabernacle and to build its earthly equivalent, the predecessor of the Jerusalem Temple. One of the principal tasks of Ezra was to impose on the population the prohibition of mixed marriages (Exod. 34:16; Deut. 7:3), and he did so with such rigor that he imposed divorce on those who had wives who could not prove their pure Israelite lineage (Ezra 9–10). As we have already seen, this was a repressive tactic used by the *Gola* against those who lived in the countryside and never experienced exile. It was a project of domination of the priestly caste imposed on the peasant base of society.

The Establishment of the Province of Judah

In the twentieth year of Artaxerxes (445 B.C.E.) the king sent to Jerusalem a certain Nehemiah, an Israelite of his confidence, with a rather broad charge. He was to rebuild the walls of Jerusalem, populate the city, and take the civil measures necessary to consolidate the region. He remained in Jerusalem until the thirty-second year of Artaxerxes (433 B.C.E.), which confirms our initial impression that he was not a commissar with a limited mission, but a governor of a new Persian province. Judah was at this time separated administratively from Samaria and given its own (Persian) government.

Even though Nehemiah had the support of the king, he encountered the opposition of the neighboring provinces for whom a strong Judah was not desirable. From the mention of the enemies of Nehemiah (in texts such as Neh. 4:1 and 6:1) we can deduce that the bordering provinces were Samaria to the north, Amon to the east, Arabia to the south, and Ashdod to the west. Of these provinces Samaria was the most affected, for it had lost part of its territory, including the Temple where some of its population still directed their pilgrimages. But the other provinces also, especially Amon, had Yahweh believers who looked to Jerusalem as a principal place of worship.

The Gerizim Temple

The letters of the Jews of Elephantine in Egypt in the year 408 show a respect for the civilian authorities both of Jerusalem and Samaria, although a recognition of the priestly authority only of Jerusalem. It was during the course of the fourth century that the inevitable happened, the building of a Yahweh temple within the province of Samaria to serve as the religious center of that province.

The historian Josephus of the first century C.E. places the authorization for this construction during the passage of Alexander through Palestine in 332 B.C.E. (*Ant.* 11§8-9; 13§9). A careful reading of these texts makes one suspect that they are artificial constructions based on an elaboration of Neh. 13:28. In any case, this construction in itself presupposes the existence of the province of Judah, which was created according to our hypothesis in 445 B.C.E., and the existence of the Pentateuch in its finished state, which was probably finished shortly before the mission of Ezra (458 B.C.E. or, if the king in Ezra 7:7 is Artaxerxes, 397 B.C.E.). The invasion of Alexander is the latest date possible (the *terminus ad quem*) for this construction, which may well have been earlier. In short, the Gerizim Temple was built some time between 445 and 332 B.C.E.

The chosen location, Mount Gerizim, a mountain facing Shechem, had the advantage of being a place with much tradition, where Joshua had gathered the tribes before his death (Joshua 24). Besides, Deuteronomy authorizes an altar on Mount Ebal, in front of Gerizim (Deut. 27:4-7), and says explicitly by name that Mount Gerizim is a mount of blessing (Deut. 11:29). Within a law book that requires one exclusive place of worship this inexplicable reference gave the Samaritan leaders a solid exegetical support for the building of their sanctuary with the claim that they were fulfilling the will of Moses by establishing a place of worship at the legitimate place that he specified. They could plausibly claim that Jerusalem was a misreading of the lawbook.

From the viewpoint of the Samaritan elite, it was indispensable to have "their" Temple. It was a political necessity. But the effect for the faith of the people was to create a religious schism, for the result was to create two contradictory interpretations of the same revealed text, the Pentateuch. To make pilgrimages to Gerizim was to reject Jerusalem as the legitimate Temple and vice versa. Moses had clearly stated (Lev. 17:1-7 and Deut. 12:1-14) that there could be only one legitimate place of worship, the place Yahweh chose among all the tribes. Thus, a political problem of the elites of Jerusalem and Samaria ended posing a problem of faith for the people, a problem that was still not resolved in the time of Jesus of Nazareth (see John 4).

The Chronistic History versus the "Deutero-Prophets"

In the course of the two centuries of Persian domination the priestly caste, which controlled the life of Judah, made a new reading of the history of Israel. The resulting work is a history of great redactional complexity, which reveals the passage through several editions and cannot be reconstructed with confidence today. It culminated in 1 and 2 Chronicles, which seem to have been completed in the fourth century before the construction of the Temple on Mount Gerizim and the consequent schism, because they show no awareness. This rereading of the history of Israel begins, after ample genealogical tables, with the death of Saul and the kingship of David, and ends with the destruction of the Temple by Nebuchadnezzar. Its main source of information is the Deuteronomistic history (Dtr), to which it adds independent information about administrative and military matters.

The center of the history of Israel, according to this rereading, is the Jerusalem Temple. It shows a great interest in the organization of the priestly and Levitical personnel that practice their trades there. Its interest in David comes from the conviction that it was this king who organized the personnel for the cultic service in Jerusalem, leaving everything in place so that his son Solomon could undertake the construction and put to work the various Levitical and priestly groups according to his instructions. David was a singer and composer of psalms, which he placed in the care of the Levitical families of Asaph, Heman, Korah, and Yeduthun to take charge of the Temple singing.

Moses had charged the Levites that they carry the ark on their shoulders (1 Chron. 15:15). When David brought the ark to Jerusalem to remain there, he assigned to the Levites a new task, that of leading the singing (1 Chron. 6:16). For this important service they were outfitted with the "spirit of Yahweh" (2 Chron. 20:14), and became prophets as a result. The story of the battle of Jehoshaphat against Amon (2 Chron. 20) illustrates the prophetic importance of the singers (2 Chron. 20:14-17). They announced victory and encouraged the troops with their songs and prophecies. In Hezekiah's reform the Levitical singers also appear as prophetic figures who guide the actions (2 Chron. 29:25-30). Heman and Asaph, fathers of Levitical families of singers, are called by the Chroniclers "seers," indicating that they had assumed prophetic functions (1 Chron. 25:5; 2 Chron. 29:30). There is a clear tendency in Chronicles for the singers of the Temple to take the place of the men of the spirit of Yahweh, the prophets. For instance, the Chronistic text (2 Chron. 34:30) puts the Levites in the place given to the prophets in 2 Kings, the source from which it draws its information on the Josianic reform (2 Kings 23:2).

The prophetic movement had been a defense for the people against the impositions of the kings and their apparatuses of domination throughout the history of Israel. Chronicles is a witness to a process of taking over this tradition by the Temple personnel, who in the Persian period were the true dominators. According to the priestly caste that exercised their power from the Temple, the true prophets were the Levitical singers who sang the word of Yahweh by inspiration. In order to understand this it is necessary to understand the aggressiveness of the popular response.

The last prophets to present themselves with their own names as messengers sent by Yahweh were Haggai and Zechariah at the time of the construction of the Second Temple (520–516 B.C.E.). Instead of being defenders of people's interests they devoted themselves to urging the people to support the project of the *Gola,* rebuilding the Temple. During the long period of Persian hegemony the true successors of the prophets went into anonymity. Believing that now the spirit of Yahweh was not moving authentic prophets, they contented themselves with studying the sayings of the ancient prophets and anonymously adding to them their own sayings. These pious and diligent successors of the great prophets are those who are known in biblical Studies as the "Deutero-Prophets." Their sayings are found in passages such as Isaiah 24–27; Jer. 23:34-40; Zechariah 9-14; Joel 3–4, and the whole book of Malachi (which is not a proper name and seems to have been composed as an annex to the book of Zechariah).

These circles were bitter toward the Levites who were calling themselves prophets and thus robbing the people of Yahweh of the memory of those who were truly prophets (Zech. 13:2-6). Anyone who dares to declare himself a prophet is a liar and must be killed by his own parents.

The spirit of Yahweh had abandoned God's people, after having guided them for so long by sending the word insistently through the prophets. Yahweh will again send the spirit in the latter times when the elders will dream dreams and the young men see visions (according to the lovely poem in Joel 3:1-5). Meanwhile, those who call themselves prophets are nothing but impostors. In this same vein, Malachi says that in the latter times, after the current drought of prophecy, Yahweh will send the prophet Elijah to prepare the people for the coming of Yahweh's salvation (Mal. 3:1, 23-24).

The contrast between Chronicles and the Deutero-Prophets is the religious expression of a class conflict, which during the time of the Persians put the humble folk of the countryside in conflict with the exiles who had returned and installed themselves in Jerusalem with the protection of the empire, claiming to be the sole legitimate heirs of the faith in Yahweh. It was an effort to steal the faith of the people, converting it into an instrument of their oppression.

13
The Hellenistic Period
332-167 B.C.E.

We can define the beginning of Hellenistic domination in Palestine in a very simple manner, by the passage of Alexander the Great through Palestine on his way to conquer Egypt. Without great difficulties he was able to subdue the Persian provinces of Palestine to his control. The ending of this period is not as well defined. The uprising of Mattathias and his sons in 167 marked the breaking out of the insurrection and its sequels known as the Maccabean War. This insurrection and war ended with the establishment of a Jewish monarchy headed by the Hasmonean family over the Jewish population of Palestine. In this manner a degree of autonomy was reached over against the Hellenistic kingdoms, a situation that still implied a considerable Seleucid (Hellenistic) influence, although the Seleucid kings were no longer able to impose their own rulers over the population. If hegemony implies a sufficient degree of consent on the part of the dominated population to make unnecessary the constant use of force to maintain the control of the dominant power, then Palestine was no longer under Hellenistic hegemony after the insurrection of 167. For this reason this chapter ends with that insurrection.

Alexander himself ruled only briefly over Palestine, because he died in Babylon in 323 B.C.E. Three of his generals disputed the vast territories Alexander had submitted to Greek control, and Palestine was one of the battlegrounds where the disputes were worked out. After a period of open conflict, Palestine was submitted to the Hellenistic kings of Egypt, the Ptolemies. During their reign, Palestine was a part of the province of "Syria and

Phoenicia." There was a stable government by four successive kings: Ptolemy I Soter (301–282), Ptolemy II Philadelphos (282–246), Ptolemy III Euergetes (246–221), and Ptolemy IV Philopator (221–203). Seleucus, a rival of Ptolemy, was able to retain the eastern part of Alexander's conquests: Persia, Babylonia, and Armenia. He established his capital in Antioch on the river Orontes, in the north of Syria where one entered these lands coming from the Mediterranean Sea. The Seleucids, Alexander's descendants, never accepted the loss of "Syria and Phoenicia" to the Ptolemies. After several fruitless attempts to reverse this situation, finally Antioch III the Great managed to defeat the Egyptian army of Ptolemy V Epiphanes at Paneas in 198 B.C.E. He was able to gain sovereignty over Syria and Phoenicia for the Seleucids, who governed the area until the uprising that broke out in 167.

The Ptolemaic domination over Palestine gave it one of the longest periods of peace in its difficult history. It was, however, a period of an economic exploitation perfected to a science. The Greeks established a strongly centralized bureaucratic state in Egypt that was more "Asiatic" than "Greek." The highest officer of each region, or *nome* of the kingdom was the general responsible for the troops stationed there, the *strategos*. At his side in the administration was the *oikonomos* responsible for finances, and especially for taxes. There was a series of other officers, but all were carefully supervised by envoys continually sent out by the central government.

All of the province of Syria and Phoenicia was regarded as territory conquered by the sword, and as such the personal property of the king, but it was not all administered in the same way. The main source of information is a certain Zeno, an envoy of Apolonios the *dioiketes*, or "second in command," of King Ptolemy II Philadelphos. There is no direct information about this period in the biblical texts, except the vision in Daniel 11, which only gives its military history in coded form. The Jews did not have any political history of their own during the Ptolemean century, and yet it was an important time insofar as the social formations it left would be maintained, with some variants, until the end of the history of Israel in the wars with Rome.

The administration of those territories in Palestine that are of interest to the history of Israel was complex; it is possible to distinguish at least three forms. The newest one and the one with the greatest long-term importance was the introduction of Hellenistic cities. Alexander or his assistant Perdiccas had already established military colonies in Samaria (in Ephraim) and Gerasa (in Transjordan). These were colonized by Macedonian soldiers to whom lands were given and, after the manner of Greek cities, a measure of self-government was recognized. The Ptolemies later founded "cities" at Acco, which received the name of Ptolemais and became the principal center of all Syria and Phoenicia, at Beth-Sean at the far eastern end of the valley of Jezreel, which received the new name of Skythopolis, Philateria near the Sea of Galilee at its southern point, Philadelphia (the ancient city of Rabbath-Amon, capital of the Ammonites), and several more on the coastal plain, among them Dor and Gaza.

These cities were colonized not only by soldiers, but also by Greeks and Hellenized persons who were civilians. They served the Ptolemies as a means of controlling the native population and also of realizing a more intense exploitation of the agricultural potential of the land. The Hellenistic city was composed of a base of free citizens who governed the affairs of their own city within the limits prescribed by the founder, who in these cases was one or another of the Ptolemies. Within the city might live a majority of persons who were not citizens, domestic and productive slaves, and foreigners who practiced various activities but who had no voice in public affairs and no right to possess land within or outside of the city in its territorial domains. The full citizen was one who lived in the city, but lived off the product of agricultural lands that were worked by slaves and wage earners. To be an owner of land it was necessary to be a citizen. Women had important functions in the administration of the properties of their husbands but no participation in public affairs.

The most important center for the reproduction of social life was the gymnasium, where young males studied with a curriculum that had for its center the epics of Homer, which exalted the military virtues, and the practice of sports, which prepared them physically and mentally for war.

Besides the cities, Palestine included vast extensions of lands of the king that were administered directly by functionaries of the Ptolemaic state or given as favors to friends of the king for their own enrichment. As it seems, the greater part of the best lands were of the latter sort, including most of the Mediterranean coastal lands, the valleys of Jezreel and Jordan, and a good share of Transjordan. Cities were founded by taking blocks of the royal lands to distribute among the citizens.

Jerusalem was considered a priestly city at the head of the Jewish *ethnos* "nation." It was not the only city of this kind in the Hellenistic kingdoms nor were the Jews the only *ethnos*. Other *ethnē* (the plural of *ethnos*) recognized in Palestine were those of the Idumeans and the Gazites. The high priest in Jerusalem was given administrative functions, with the advice of a council of notables called the *gerousia* (in the time of Herod they received the name of Sanhedrin, with which readers of the Christian Bible are familiar).

The high priest was responsible for raising large sums of money for the state and had very little administrative autonomy. Nobody in Ptolemaic Palestine had much autonomy. The Ptolemaic state was a huge bureaucracy and, it seems, a highly efficient one.

Under Ptolemaic administration Syria and Phoenicia were converted into a very rich and productive agricultural region. The existing peace was surely a benefit recognized by the population. Nevertheless, the impact of the system on the daily life of the population was great. The new mode of agricultural production, especially in the lands that now belonged to the cities, destroyed the traditional life of the villages and proletarianized the native peasants. They were transformed from free agriculturalists whose immediate superiors were the elders of their villages into wage earners on land in alien hands, with no say in public affairs. The situation in the lands submitted to Jerusalem may have been better. It is also possible that the territories of the king allowed a measure of survival for the life-style of the villages. Nevertheless, to a degree that grew with the following centuries the countryside was submitted to cities of landholders who had been brought from other lands and who had no knowledge or appreciation for the traditional law of the people of Israel.

Another disturbing element in the life of the Jewish society of the period was recruitment for the army. Young Jews proved to be very good soldiers. Some were certainly recruited by force, but it is likely that a majority entered the army voluntarily, in effect, as mercenaries. The Greeks had the best armies in the world, both because of their equipment and their discipline, and the military life offered an attractive alternative to many young men whose families had recently lost their lands and control over their own economic and social practices.

Ecclesiasticus, or the Wisdom of Jesus ben Sira

The only biblical text that can be placed with confidence in the Hellenistic period is the Ecclesiasticus, a magnificent literary production that reflects the serenity and confidence with which the Jewish aristocracy could face the difficulties of the period. The author appears to have been a contemporary of the high priest Simon II, whose high priesthood covered approximately 220 to 195 B.C.E. His work is a reflection on *hokma*, "wisdom," and it is hence necessary to place it within the Israelite reflections of wisdom.

The first collections of proverbial wisdom in Israel are those found in Proverbs 10–31. These collections were probably made in the period before the destruction of Jerusalem in circles close to the Jerusalem royal court. Their authorship is pseudonymous; all or almost all are attributed to Solomon, who, according to the tradition, was a great admirer and practitioner of wisdom.

These proverbs, some of which originally came from popular sources, understand that wisdom is acquired through the careful observation of life—family, social, animal, and vegetable. It is a secular knowledge, for even though it allows a place for Yahweh the true God, it does not allow the Yahweh traditions to dominate over the observations we would call empirical. In these proverbs there is a confidence that a moral order exists in society, which rewards the one who is honest and hardworking and penalizes the one who lives in a contrary fashion. If it is true that the evidence is not always clear that all goes well for the just, the wise can confidently ask of the just one that he or she suffer patiently, because soon the wicked one will fall from the precarious heights where he or she is temporarily seated.

A time came in the social life of Israel when various social disorders shook the foundations of this confidence. In Israelite reflection, wisdom became ever more problematic. It was no longer possible to ask the "son" to diligently observe his surroundings to discover wisdom there. Wisdom became hidden and more difficult to find than the silver for which miners dig in the depths of the earth (Job 28). It was in this situation of the absence of wisdom that a lover of wisdom wrote that marvelous book of Job. Here a test case is imagined of a man who is righteous in the eyes of God and of his fellows, whom God and Satan propose to push to the extremity of misery in order tc discover the limits of his faith (in God, but also, and fundamentally, in wisdom). The protagonist of the action ends by questioning the presence of wisdom in creation, in the sphere of human relations, and even in the actions of God. It is only he as a person who maintains right—and in the end God recognizes that this is so (in a rather indirect fashion, see Job 42:7-9)!

The same social crisis is reflected in the proverbial collection preserved in Proverbs 1–9. Wisdom here takes on a life of her own. No longer is she present in the social and natural worlds where any young person might find her if he or she observes the world with attention. Wisdom is with God, and by means of wisdom God created the world (Prov. 8:22-31). She walks the streets calling on men to come to her or, alternatively, to invite her in. She must take the initiative in a world where her presence is no longer evident at every turn (Prov. 8:1-11). She builds a house, sets a table, and goes out to look for guests (Prov. 9:1-6).

It is difficult, in fact impossible, to date the social crisis that appears in Job and Proverbs 1–9. We may suppose that it was after the destruction of the state institutions of Samaria (722) and Jerusalem (586). There is no need to place them later that the sixth century, but no reason either to deny that they might come from the Persian period.

On the other hand, Qoheleth of Ecclesiastes gives evidence of Persian influence in its vocabulary and, some think, also of Greek. It also reveals the same social crisis of wisdom that we found in Job and Proverbs 1–9. For Qoheleth, writing under the name of King Solomon, life is absurd. "Vanity of vanities; all is vanity" (Qoh. 1:2). It is absurd to think that the wise and the fool come to the same end; as the fool dies, so does the wise one (Qoh. 2:15-16). Wisdom is the greatest of all possessions (Qoh. 7:11-12), and it wounds reason that all the effort expended in acquiring wisdom should come inevitably to nought, for "a living dog is better than a dead lion" (Qoh. 9:4). When one labors to acquire riches one has the benefit of enjoying pleasures, but it is absurd that one must leave them to others (Qoh. 6:1-2). Qoheleth refuses to give up on the faith (or hope or desire) that there is wisdom in the world; his "vanity of vanities, all is vanity" is a protest against the absence of wisdom where his reason tells him that there ought to be wisdom. He is a teacher, and he writes and teaches so that his disciples may not be satisfied with this absurd world, and yet, he has no remedy. . . .

And after this trajectory of celebration of wisdom, the removal of wisdom to the higher spheres, and lament or protest over the absence of wisdom, we come to Jesus ben Sira in the apocryphal Ecclestiasticus. If Burton L. Mack's elegant reading is correct, the son of Sira writes to construct an image of wisdom who has again found her home in the world ("again" because Job, Proverbs 1–9, and Qoheleth or Ecclesiastes experienced the absence more than the presence of wisdom, after the days when the original proverbs incited youth to see wisdom in the workings of the world around them). According to the hymn to wisdom in Ecclesiasticus 24, she wandered over the earth seeking a home until God told her to settle in Jerusalem, and there she found her rest, teaching the law of God to God's people.

After gathering reflections on the multiple facets of human life in a long series of chapters, this wise man finishes his work with a great celebration of the glory of God revealed in nature (Ecclus. 42:15-43:33) and in the history of Israel (Ecclus. 44–50). The latter is a new reading of the history of Israel as the search for the glory and wisdom of the institutions and alliances in which to become incarnate, which culminates surprisingly in the perfection of the beauty of the high priest Simon officiating in the Temple in his splendid garments. Here in worship wisdom found her place on earth in the midst of the people of Israel. Our astonishment is due no doubt to our knowledge that the world of Jesus ben Sira would be shattered with the Maccabean rebellion only a few years later. Before it was destroyed it was sullied by the sale of the high priesthood to the highest bidder, the Seleucid kings being the sellers and various priests the bidders. Excepting its lack of permanence, ben Sira's is a handsome proposal, which shows how much sense of security the Jews had achieved during the long peace of the Ptolemies. The wise person had no way to foresee how short-lived this glory would be. It was an elitist project without a stable base in the welfare of the majority of the people.

The Hellenizing Project

A certain Tobias, a member of a distinguished Jewish family in Transjordan, the name of which was derived from the place Tab'el at the time of Isaiah, lived in Jerusalem and was a great landholder in the middle of the third century B.C.E. His son Joseph was a businessman who for twenty-two years, 239–217 B.C.E., contracted with King Ptolemy III Euergetes the collecting of taxes for the whole province of Syria and Phoenicia. Joseph was possibly the richest man in the province. His mother, the wife of Tobias, was a sister of the high priest Onias. This information, which reaches us by means of the historian Josephus, is confirmed by the Zeno papyri. It is important in that it reveals the degree to which the principal Jewish families were integrated into the Hellenistic world.

During the government of Antiochus IV Epiphanes (175–163 B.C.E.) the principal priests made an effort to found a Hellenistic city in Jerusalem named Antioch in Jerusalem. Their promoter was the high priest Jason (a Greek name), who had bought the post by offering to the king an increase of taxes and a generous initial sum of eighty talents. With this offer Antiochus removed the high priest Onias III and recognized Jason, a brother to Onias. The conservatives, who resisted the Hellenizing project, rested their case on a "letter of liberty" by Antiochus, which allowed the Jewish *ethnos* to live according to their ancestral laws. Jason, supported as it seems by a majority of the priests in Jerusalem, responded by establishing the *polis,* complete with a gymnasium. Jason and his group controlled access to citizenship in the new city. The laws of the city, which became automatically the laws of the Jews, were "democratically" established as was the Greek custom, thus undercutting the position of the conservatives.

The level of corruption to which life had sunk is illustrated by the fact that three years later Menelaos "bought" the high priesthood through raising the annual taxes he promised by 300 talents. The Seleucids, who took control of Palestine by conquest in 198, were not able to manage the excellent administrative system left by the Ptolemies through which they had extracted great quantities of tribute. Instead, they resorted to opportunistic measures like the sale of the high priesthood to cover their permanent deficits. This was the setting for the insurrection that we know as the Maccabean War, with which a new period of the history of Israel began.

14
The Maccabean Insurrection and the Hasmonean Kingdom 167–163 B.C.E.

Between 167 and 63 B.C.E. the history of Israel was dominated by the activity of the dynamic family of the Hasmoneans who first led the Israelites in their rebellion against the oppressive laws of the Seleucids, which attacked the law of God, and later conquered all the territories of the ancient kingdoms of Israel and Judah. Their achievements were truly surprising. It is amazing that such a small people was able to conquer all Palestine and impose in the whole territory the Deuteronomic ideal of the recognition of the Temple of Jerusalem as the site of worship for the true God. It was possible only by means of constant wars carried out by armies that were made up at first of volunteers who fought for the restoration of the faith of Israel, but later of paid soldiers. Unfortunately, all this brave and pious patriotism took a high price in the internal division of the people, a division that found religious expression just as the nationalism had found religious expression. When the Roman legions under Pompey appeared in 65 B.C.E., they were initially welcomed by groups who were tired of the Hasmonean kings—among them the Pharisees.

The Hasmoneans were Levitical priests but not descendents of Aaron. Their original home was Modein on the western slope of the central mountain chain in Palestine. All this means that according to the last speech of Moses (Deuteronomy) they had the full right to officiate in the priestly sacrificial cultus if they went to Jerusalem, the city that was the only legitimate place of the worship of Yahweh according to Dtr's reading of Deuteronomy. Nevertheless, the dispositions of the first Sinaitic revelation (the sections we attribute to P) limited the priesthood to the descendants of Aaron, thereby excluding families like that of the Hasmoneans. In 152 when the Hasmoneans took the high priesthood for themselves, a post that was considered the head of the nation, the question of their priestly legitimacy became one of the motives for division. The Aaronite families, who since the sixth century had controlled the priesthood and had produced a literature that supported their monopoly ("P," the Chronicler's history), opposed the Hasmonean pretensions. Others of a less elitist sort, like the Essenes and the Pharisees, arose as protest movements. The difficult question of this period is, Who really represented the people's interests? Because the whole political debate was carried out as a debate about the correct interpretation of the texts, which by this time nobody doubted were inspired by God, none tried to justify their group's position in terms of popular interests.

The Political History

We have already seen the greed and opportunism of the Seleucid monarchy. These qualities were fully manifested when Antiochus IV Epiphanes sacked the Temple at Jerusalem upon his return from an Egyptian campaign in 169 B.C.E. (1 Macc. 1:16-28). Two years later he returned to Jerusalem, sacked and burned it, and built in its midst an Accra, a fortified citadel that would play an important role in the coming events (1 Macc. 1:29-35). He consecrated the Jerusalem Temple to Olympian Zeus and that of Gerizim to Hospitable Zeus (Zeus Xenios, 2 Macc. 6:1-2). Over the altar of holocausts he placed what Daniel and 1 Maccabees call the "Abomination of Desolations" (1 Macc. 1:54; Dan. 9:27), probably a statue of Zeus. This was probably a response to a request from the Hellenizing sector among the priests, for thus we can understand what is said about "the inhabitants of the place" (2 Macc. 6:2). In their desire to be truly cosmopolitan, they would have seen in Zeus a manifestation of the same Yahweh who created heaven and earth. Olympian Zeus was conceived by the Greeks as king of the universe; this could be and apparently was interpreted as another name for Yahweh.

Antiochus decreed a prohibition against the circumcision of children and ordained the celebration of his own birthday (2 Macc. 6:3-11). Faced with what he and a sector of the Jewish population saw as open provocations, Mattathias responded with violence in Modein. He killed a Jew on the altar who made an offensive sacrifice and also the envoy of the king who officiated (1 Macc. 2:24-25). He then fled to the hills with his sons and other brave followers, and began a struggle against the Greeks and the Jews who violated the law of God.

A Chronology of the Hasmonean Leadership in Judea

167 Mattathias rebels, killing the Jewish renegade in Modein.

166–160 Judas, the third son of Mattathias, fights for independence. The Temple worship is restored to purity in 164. Judas Maccabeaus and his brothers campaign in Galilee and Gilead, destroying Greek cities. (Alcimus, an Aaronite, is named high priest, 162–159.)

160–143 Jonathan, a brother of Judas, assumes the leadership in the fight. Jonathan declares himself high priest, 152.

143–134 Simon, another brother, becomes "high priest, general, and leader of the Jews." Simon recaptures the Accra of Jerusalem, 141. Territorial expansion, including the port of Joppe.

134–104 John Hyrcanus assumes the titles of his father. He destroys the Temple of Gerizim. He conquers Samaria (107) and Idumea, where he forces circumcision on the population.

104–103 The government of Aristobulus I.

103–76 Alexander Jannaeus, another son of John Hyrcanus, declares himself high priest and king. He conquers all of Transjordan, and the plain of Acco or Ptolemais. He names Antipater I *strategos* of Idumea.

76–67 Salome Alexandra, widow of Alexander Jannaeus, becomes queen, and her son Hycanus II high priest.

67–63 Aristobulus II, another son of Alexander and Salome, takes on both titles (king and high priest).

65 Syria becomes a Roman province.

63 Pompey conquers Jerusalem.

63–40 Hyrcanus II becomes high priest again.

55–43 The Idumean Antipater II becomes procurator of Palestine.

47–40 Hyrcanus II is recognized as ethnarch of Judea, Galilee, and Perea.

40–37 Antigonus, the last of the Hasmonean rulers, is king and high priest.

Mattathias and his followers destroyed pagan altars, killed Jews who followed the new practices, and circumcised children by force. Mattathias died of natural causes in 166 B.C.E., but his struggle continued and was deepened under the leadership of his third son, Judas, who was known by his nickname Maccabaeus, "hammer." The Seleucids sent an army to restore order, but to their astonishment, Judas and his army were able to defeat them at Beth Horon (1 Macc. 3:24). The following year, 165 B.C.E., a Seleucid army invaded from the south and again Judas defeated them, this time at Beth Shur on the southern border of Judah. The following year Judas was able to take the city of Jerusalem, although the Greeks held the Accra. On the twenty-fifth of Kislev, in the midst of general rejoicing, the Temple was purified and worship reinstated there (1 Macc. 4.36ff).

It was quite an achievement, but the Jewish forces did not rest. In 163 Judas and his brothers made incursions in Galilee and Gilead, both regions where many Israelites lived who had never stopped believing in Yahweh in all the generations since the destruction of the kingdom of Israel. The Jewish army destroyed several Hellenistic cities, so that their inhabitants fled into exile to escape the sword. Judas brought to Jerusalem and Judah all the Israelites who wished to take refuge under the Hasmonean project (1 Macc. 5:9-54, especially vss. 42-45). The Jewish forces were defeated at Beth Zechariah, and the Hellenistic king offered peace on the basis of the cancellation of the Hellenizing program that had provoked the uprising. Tired of war, the people accepted (1 Macc. 6:60), and the king named a priest from a good Aaronic family, Alcimus.

It was a decisive moment. The immediate objectives of the insurrection had been accomplished. The king had canceled his humiliating program and promised to return to the *status quo ante.* In the face of this opportunity, the people divided. The "Hasideans," pious persons given to keeping the law, accepted Alcimus and promoted peace among the people (1 Macc. 7:12-14), but Judas with another group stayed on the war path, sweeping over the land "to take vengeance of the deserters" (1 Macc. 7:24). Alcimus had to flee and Judas again obtained some victories, although he fell finally in the midst of the defeat of his army in 160 B.C.E.

The death of Judas Maccabaeus did not mean the end of his struggle to restore Palestine to the control of Jerusalem and the law of Moses. His brother Jonathan took charge, and later (152 B.C.E.) proclaimed himself high priest, with the recognition of the Seleucid king, or, more precisely, the recognition of one of the claimants to the Seleucid throne (1 Macc. 10:18). It was a step that alienated another block of the faithful, those who clung to the Aaronic rules for the priesthood. Besides the opposition of the elites, there arose, probably at this time, the movement of the Essenes among people of more humble origins.

These people withdrew into "convents" where they lived their lives in community centered around work and the study of the Bible as they waited for the restoration of the true priesthood. They were led by a certain "righteous teacher" or "teacher of righteousness" in their devotion to the study of the Scriptures, putting the emphasis on the prophets, where they searched for clues to the events of the latter days.

From 152, when Jonathan took over the high priesthood, the nation was divided into factions that had the appearance of religious sects. They fought over the true interpretation of one and the same religious tradition. Both civil and religious power remained in the hands of the Hasmoneans until the invasion of Pompey and the fall of Jerusalem in 63 B.C.E. They had the clear intention of restoring the nation Israel to the Davidic model. Evidence suggests that they had a broad popular support in this. The Hasideans and Pharisees did not accept the need to fight for national power but rather were content to stress the need for strict adherence to the law of Sinai. They had broken with the Hasmoneans over the peace of 160, and were not reconciled until the reign of Salome Alexandra (76–67 B.C.E.). Their strength is reflected in the political importance of this reconciliation and the Hasmoneans' need of resorting the mercenaries in their armies. The third group after the Hasmoneans and their followers and the Pharisees is that of the Essenes, for whom is it hard to determine how much popular support they enjoyed for their policy of withdrawal.

Jonathan's success in advancing the project of restoring ancient Israelite boundaries can be seen in King Demetrius's recognition of his control over three districts that had traditionally belonged not to Judah but to Samaria, Aphairema, Lydda, and Rathamin (1 Macc. 11:34).

Simon, another son of Mattathias, succeeded Jonathan in the Hasmonean government from 143 to 134 B.C.E. He took the titles of "high priest, general, and leader of the Jews" (1 Macc. 13:42). He acted increasingly like a king, as when he entered into treaties with Sparta and Rome (1 Macc. 14:16-24). He was able to reconquer the Accra of Jerusalem, throw out its inhabitants (including, we suppose, the Seleucid military garrison), and "purify its pollutions" (1 Macc. 13:49-53). He directed several military campaigns, during one of which he was able to take the most important port city of the Palestinian coast at this time, Joppe, thus giving the Hasmonean kingdom an opening to the sea (1 Macc. 14:4-6).

Simon's son John Hyrcanus (134–104 B.C.E.) succeeded him. He extended his dominions to Shechem, where he destroyed the temple of the Samaritans on Mount Gerizim. He conquered Idumea to the south of Judah, obligating its population to submit to circumcision and to the whole law of Moses (Josephus, *Ant.* 13§254–58). His son Alexander Janneaus (103–76 B.C.E.), now with the title of king, completed the conquest of Palestine with the submission under his rule of all of Transjordan, Moab, and Gilead, as well as the Phoenician port of Acco and its coastal plain. The Hasmonean dynasty ended with his wife Salome Alexandra (76–67 B.C.E.) and two sons who disputed power until the Romans invaded. Under Alexander Janneaus and Salome Alexander the governor of Idumea was Antipas, whose family played a major role in the life of Judah later.

This quick summary, which omits many bribes and assassinations within the Hasmonean family, allows one to appreciate something of the glory of the Hasmonean national liberation, as well as the ambition, corruption, and tragedy that marked this period. It was Hasmonean policy to restore the religion of Yahweh by the force of arms. They enjoyed considerable popular support. From the viewpoint of the people the most important accomplishment of their administration was the destruction of the Hellenistic cities. These were returned by force to the nation that was governed from Jerusalem by the high priest of Yahweh (who also happened to be king). The city that would not accept these terms, which were contrary to Greek customs, was destroyed and its inhabitants run through by the sword, as happened to Pella in the times of Alexander Janneaus (Josephus *Ant.* 13§397).

The Literature of the Hasmonean Period

The heroic acts and the tragedies of the Hasmonean nationalist and religious project evoked several literary works of importance, although only one (Daniel) entered without controversy into the collection of books recognized as inspired by the rabbis who determined such matters. The books that were produced among the Jews of Palestine (we exclude here the Judaism of the dispersion, whose life is tangential to the history of Israel) were two history books (1 and 2 Maccabees), two apocalyptic books (Daniel and the first parts in the long redactional history of the Apocalypse of Enoch), one priestly rereading of the history of the patriarchs (Jubilees), and several documents of the Essene communities, among which the most important are the Damascus Document and the Manual of Discipline. Besides these, we know about other books that have not survived.

First Maccabees is preserved only in Greek, although its original language was Hebrew. It is not part of the Hebrew canon of Scripture, although it entered Christian Bibles because Christians used the Greek Scriptures (Septuagint, LXX). Protestant churches have always had reservations about its canonicity. It is a sober history book. It relates the events that transpired from the crowning of Antiochus IV Epiphanes (175 B.C.E.) until the beginning of the reign of the Hasmonean John Hyrcanus (134 B.C.E.). It is written in the assurance that it was Yahweh who restored God's people, acting in history for their salvation as in the ancient times of Moses. It is, however, sober and reserved in its presentation of the acts of God, avoiding miraculous interventions that probably seemed to its authors distinctive only of the ancient times.

Second Maccabees has a clear didactic intention of celebrating the actions of God and also those of the heroes and martyrs like Judas Maccabeaus and the old man Eleazar, who preferred torture and death to contaminating himself with the flesh of pigs (2 Macc. 6:18-31). This book contents itself with telling the story of the glorious days of Judas, and does not continue with his successors. Its story of the martyrdom of the seven brothers (2 Maccabees 7) exhorts others to follow martyrdom rather than to disobey the law, and clearly poses its confidence in a bodily resurrection, at least for martyrs.

The two books of Maccabees were written within the circles close to the Hasmonean project. In contrast, Daniel was written during the years of the glorious struggle in which the cause was to restore the purity of the Temple, between 167 and 164 B.C.E. Daniel stands back from the fight of Judas; it believes the outcome of history is decided in heaven. There is little that human creatures can do to hurry the historical calendar God has proposed. Both the dream of Nebuchadnezzar (Dan. 2:31-45) and the vision of the four beasts (Dan. 7:1-14) view history in its full sweep as a whole from the perspective of its end, which will be the full government of God, removing from the earthly scene the empires of the past, present, and future. Even though the allegory of Daniel 11 shows that the authors viewed with keen interest the events of contemporary history, they did not see the people of God as a major factor in the history. Their salvation would come, rather, by means of "Michael, the great prince who defends the sons of your people" (Dan. 12:1). In other words, Daniel is evidence that even during the period of greatest glory, victory, and unity, there were sectors of the nation who took their distance from the struggle, in the hope that salvation would come from heaven.

The broad Enoch literature, which is only preserved in total in Ethiopic, arose also in circles who looked at the historical scene in an apocalyptic key. Only the oldest parts of this literature come from the Hasmonean period. Its importance is that it reinforces Daniel's witness to the existence of sectors of the people who separated themselves from the political fight for the recovery of national independence.

The Essene writings allow us to know a sector of the people who took their faith so seriously that they withdrew to the desert to keep pure as they hoped for the restoration of the Temple to its legitimate priests. We have already indicated that the "teacher of justice" probably took his disciples to the desert at the time when Jonathan assumed the high priesthood (152 B.C.E.). Jubilees, which is not part of the Bible as it was accepted later, gives witness to the existence of another priestly group that was not content with the Hasmonean leadership of the religious life of Israel.

Conclusion

From the viewpoint of the poor people, and especially the poor people of Galilee and Gilead who considered themselves devotees of Yahweh, the most important thing that the Hasmoneans did was to destroy the Hellenistic cities that the Ptolemies had founded. Unfortunately, our sources do not inform us about the agrarian policies followed by the Hasmoneans in the lands recovered from these cities. Therefore we do not know what happened to the peasants who during the previous century had been forced to become wage earners on alien lands. From the first years, the days of Judas, we read that many were taken to Judah from Galilee and Gilead for their protection, but we do not know how they were included in Judean society.

15
The Roman Domination 63 B.C.E. to 135 C.E.

We now arrive at the last chapter of the history of this nation of peasants who wished to be free under the sole sovereignty of Yahweh their God. Throughout the centuries of their existence, we have seen how the original project was subverted by dominant sectors that were able to take advantage of foreign pressures to impose themselves over the peasant sector. In a critical moment of the history, towards the end of the sixth century and throughout the fifth, the *Gola* was able to impose an elitist priestly project with the support of the Persian Empire. The ancient organization of peasants in their villages led by counsels of elders was struck a heavy blow in the third century by the foundation in Palestinian territory of cities on the Hellenistic style and by the introduction of the private ownership of the land. In the second century there was a nationalist reaction led by a sector of the Levitical (not Aaronite) priesthood, which reached a surprising success in the attempt to return to the Deuteronomist model that Josiah had attempted with less success in the seventh century. All of this has prepared us to understand the last two centuries of Israel, from 63 B.C.E. to 135 C.E., two centuries of intense popular struggles, which ended in the violent death of Israel under the brutal repression of the Roman legions. What would survive the tragedy in Israel was the diaspora, a great religious community scattered throughout the world, uprooted from the soil and the peasant existence that had been the essence of the Israelite project. Another survivor of the tragedy was yet another religious community, the Christian church, which like the Jewish diaspora also traced its ancestry to Israel, and also lost its peasant roots. The story of the glory and the tragedy of the end of Israel occupy us in this last portion of our story.

Historical writings allow us to reconstruct the events of this period in some detail. These are the several historical works of Flavius Josephus, an Israelite from a priestly family with sympathy for the Romans. He gave himself the name Flavius after the Flavian emperors Vespasian (69–79 C.E.) and Titus (79–81 C.E.). Josephus was born in 37 C.E. and lived until the last years of the first century. He was an active participant in the First War, having been named general of the revolutionary forces by the provisional government of the high priest Ananus with the charge of directing the campaign in Galilee. This campaign ended with the decisive defeat at Jotpata (67 C.E.) and Josephus's capture by the Romans. Before the fall of Jerusalem, when Vespasian was named Emperor, Josephus was released and treated with respect by the Romans. After the war was over, a statue of Josephus was erected in Rome! It is a matter of debate whether the historian should be considered a traitor. He considered himself a seer who, like the prophets of olden days, had foreseen that God would turn Israel over into the hands of Rome. He foretold the appointment of Vespasian as Emperor in a vision he had before the battle of Jotpata in which he himself was the losing general. His writings make it clear that he never had any sympathy with the popular uprising. If he accepted the charge of the Galilean campaign it was to avoid allowing it to fall to the radicals. His intention, like that of the provisional government that named him, was to achieve a negotiated peace with Rome that would satisfy the radicals (the popular movement) without fundamentally altering the standing social relations.

With the war behind him, in the years 75–79 C.E., Josephus wrote the *Jewish Wars*, a history of the war in seven books (*J.W.*). It is a most valuable testimony by a participant of the events, even if it is anything but impartial for that reason. Later, in the last decade of the first century, he wrote an immense historical work in twenty books known as the *Jewish Antiquities* (*Ant.*), which tells the history of Israel from its origins to the beginning of the war. In addition, he wrote two shorter works, a *Life* and an apology *Against Apion* (*Ag. Ap.*). In their totality these writings are the principal source for any history of Israel during this period. To them we must add the information that can be gathered from the Christian gospels and the traditions of the rabbis gathered around the year 200 C.E. in the Mishnah.

A Chronology of Roman Domination Over Palestine

63 B.C.E. Pompey conquers Jerusalem

37–4 B.C.E. Herod rules as king over all of Palestine (minus the cities of the Decapolis). At the time of his death, the kingdom is divided among his three sons:

- 4 B.C.E.–6 C.E. Archelaus, ethnarch of Judea, Idumea, and Samaria;
- 4 B.C.E.–39 C.E. Herod Antipas, tetrarch of Galilee and Perea;
- 4 B.C.E.–34 C.E. Philip, tetrarch of Trachonitis, Batanea, and Auranitis.

Archelaus is deposed and Judea made into a province under Roman procurators named by the senate:

- 6–9 C.E. Copponius
- 9–12 C.E. Ambibulus
- 12–15 C.E. Rufus
- 15–26 C.E. Valerius Gratus
- 26–37 C.E. Pontius Pilate
- 36 C.E. Marcellus
- 37–41 C.E. Marullus.

37–44 C.E. Agrippa I, a grandson of Herod, was made king over the tetrarchy of Philip in 37, over Galilee and Perea in 40, and Judea in 41.

Palestine again became a province ruled by procurators:

44–46 C.E. Cuspius Fadus
46–48 C.E. Tiberius Alexander
48–52 C.E. Ventidius Cumanus
52–60 C.E. Felix
60–62 C.E. Agrippa II, a son of Festus
62–64 C.E. Agrippa I, is king of Albinus
64–66 C.E. several districts, mainly Florus
49–92 C.E. Hellenistic, in the north of Palestine.

66–74 C.E. The First Great War with Rome

66–67 C.E. Provisional government under the high priest Ananus

67 C.E. Defeat at Jotpata

67–70 C.E. Radical control of Jerusalem

70 C.E. Titus destroys the city

74 C.E. The fortress Massada falls to the Roman legions

74–132 C.E. Leadership of the Jamnia Sanhedrin

74–80 C.E. Prince Johanan ben Zakkai

80–120 C.E. Prince Gamaliel II

132–135 C.E. The Second Great War with Rome

135 C.E. Fall of Bethar

The Imperial Administration

During the two hundred years of Roman domination over Israel up to its definitive disappearance there were many administrative changes in the region, which are reflected only in part in the chronological chart above. Throughout these changes it is possible to discern some tendencies, which we shall try to clarify in this section.

One of the chief Roman concerns in this region was the defense of the eastern frontier of the Empire. Throughout this period the principal enemies of Rome in the east were the Parthians beyond the Euphrates River. Closer to Israel, the Arabs also offered occasional opposition. The Roman alliance with Herod and his sons can be explained by the advantages he offered for defense, thus permitting the release of military units that otherwise would have been committed to Palestine. Herod was Idumean and hence a "native" to the region; he knew the Romans and was completely loyal to them; and he enjoyed a fragile legitimacy by means of his marriage to Mariamne of the family of the Hasmoneans.

Nevertheless, it was not in the Roman interests to allow a centralization of power in the hands of their subjects, so they viewed Herod's large kingdom in Palestine as a temporary phenomenon. The well-known maxim *divide et impera* was applied in the region. In the first place, the Romans encouraged the founding and strengthening of Hellenistic cities. These cities enjoyed autonomy, which in practice meant that their relations with the higher Roman authorities were direct and not through the local government. Besides, in the cities there was the private property of land, which always destroyed the cohesion of the peasant villages—this rested on the communal possession of productive lands. The peasants, not being citizens, lacked any right to be landowners and were forced to seek salaried work if they stayed on the land, or else to emigrate in search of other means of subsistence without the security of their ties to the community and the land. Property rights were the heart of Roman views of society and they favored cities.

In those areas where it proved difficult to found cities, either because of the unfavorable topographic characteristics or the resistance of the population, such as in Galilee (its central mountains, not so the Jordan Valley or the Sea of Gennesareth), the Romans established governments based on ethnic groups. This was a way of deepening the divisions among the subject population, taking advantage of "natural" divisions like that dividing Judeans and Idumeans, or seeking to create new divisions where the people did not feel them, like the divisions between Judeans and Galileans, which the latter never fully accepted because of their attachment to the Temple of God in Jerusalem, an attachment acquired during the Hasmonean period.

One of the goals of the empire in its control over the territory and the population of Palestine was to extract wealth, which was realized through a complex system of tributes and taxes. There were taxes on the land, taxes on the population, customs duties, and tolls for the use of bridges and roads. To collect taxes was a business that was granted in contracts to large businessmen who in turn employed local tax collectors. For the Jewish population of Palestine there were additional taxes of the Temple, mainly the tithe on the produce of the land, and the annual tax of the didrachma on every male. The burden for the common peasant must have been very heavy.

We can represent the social structure of the period in a simplified manner by means of the following diagram:

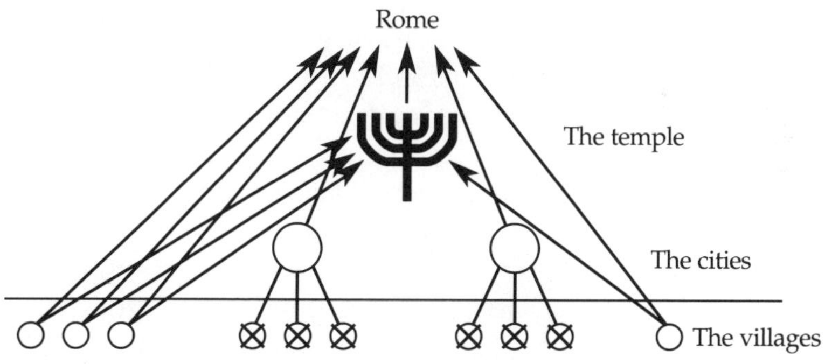

Diagram 13

The Empire extracted wealth from Palestine by three routes indicated in the diagram: (1) directly, by means of tax collectors who took tribute from the population; (2) by means of the city councils, which were obligated to make contributions for various services which the state offered; (3) through the Temple, the income of which was controlled by the Roman authorities.

The circles at the base of diagram 13 represent the traditional peasant villages subjected to a double exploitation from the Temple and from the Roman authorities. The villages that suffered the misfortune of falling within the sphere of influence of the cities, which were founded in increasing numbers throughout this period, saw how their lands were expropriated to become the patrimony of the citizens who now cultivated the newly privatized lands by means of stewards, slaves, and salaried labor. This is the dominant system we know from the parables of Jesus in the Christian gospels.

It was during the long reign of Herod the Idumean (37–4 B.C.E.) that the contours of Roman Palestine took shape. Herod ruled over all the territory that had been ruled by the Hasmoneans by virtue of his able management of his relations with Rome. He was a protégé of Antony during the triumvirate of Antony, Lepidus, and Octavian (43–37 B.C.E.), but he was able to transfer his loyalties to Octavian when he defeated Antony in 31 B.C.E. and was proclaimed Emperor Augustus by the senate.

Herod was an Idumean, and thus a Jew, although of only recent memory. During his reign he acted like a Jew with his Jewish subjects, avoiding acts in their towns that would offend their sensibilities. Nevertheless, he was also the founder of many Hellenistic cities, where he built gymnasiums, and whose avenues he adorned with statues and other works that were pagan to Jewish eyes. Among the cities he founded was the magnificent port of Ceasarea, with urban and docking facilities that made it the most comfortable city of Palestine. This was the place where later Roman procurators established their residence. It had an immense system of breakers to create a protected docking area for shipping and an ingenious system of sewers flushed by the tides of the sea.

In Jerusalem Herod started the work on a newly remodeled, amplified, and adorned Temple on a grand scale. Its splendor surpassed anything known at the time in Palestine. In addition, he built a palace for his own use in the city and the fortress Antonia, which overlooked the Temple area. Outside the city he built an amphitheater.

Herod converted Samaria into a city with the new name of Sebaste. He built fortresses at strategic points in the land, among them Massada in the desert to the west of the Dead Sea.

Even such a partial listing as this causes surprise. Such an ambitious plan of construction was only possible with a tremendous tax burden on the population. This long reign of ostentatious luxury helps explain the buildup of a broad popular resentment. After Herod's death (4 B.C.E.) and until the destruction of the people of Israel as a peasant nation (135 C.E.) there was a long popular struggle that marks the end of the history of Israel in a glory and heroism outstanding even in the glorious and heroic history of this people.

The "Philosophies" of the Jews

Josephus says that among the Jews there were three philosophies (*J.W.* 2§119ff.). Considering the numbers of the adherents that he estimates for each of them (Pharisees, "more than six thousand" [*Ant.* 17§42], Essenes "more than four thousand" [*Ant.* 18§20] and Sadducees "just a few" [*Ant.* 18§17]), one can see that the great majority of the population belonged to none of them. From Josephus's description of these philosophies (*Ant.* 18§119–166), it is clear that these were more or less disciplined groups (the Essenes more, the Sadducees less) who based their life-style on their interpretation of the same Scriptures. The Sadducees were an aristocratic group based almost exclusively at the Temple. The Essenes and the Pharisees had a closer contact with the people and from their life-styles it is possible to infer that they arose from among the middle layers of society. The Pharisees, with their teaching of a way of life that was measured by personal fidelity to the law of God, made a deep and lasting impression on the Judaism of the Diaspora which was forced to live outside the land.

Josephus admits (*Ant.* 18) the recent appearance of a "fourth philosophy" introduced by Judas, a Gaulanite from Gamala (to the east of the Sea of Galilee), a philosophy that had caused many tumults and disturbances in Palestine. Judas arose on the occasion of the census of Quirinius, governor of Syria, (6 C.E.) preaching that to submit to the census was tantamount to submitting to slavery. He did not shy away from murder to achieve his purposes (*Ant.* 18§5). He taught that there ought to be no mortal lords (*thnetous despotas*) alongside God (*J.W.* 2§118).

How are we to understand this "fourth philosophy," which Josephus does not name except to mention Judas "the Galilean" as its founder? It is obvious that the historian, in spite of feeling no sympathy for him, attributes to him a great importance for the events that led the nation to a war against Rome, which Josephus considered stupid and suicidal. During the war, sixty years later (66–74 C.E.), we find among the radical leaders a certain Menahem, the son or grandson of Judas, which suggests a measure of continuity in the disturbances that marked this period. Nevertheless, during the defense of Jerusalem at the peak of the war (67–70 C.E.) we find five radical factions that were rivals in the pursuit of revolutionary leadership: Sicarii, Zealots, Idumeans, and followers of John of Gischala and Simon bar Giora (*J.W.* 5§248–50). None of these bands can be traced directly to Judas.

It seems then that the fourth philosophy was not a sect or an organized revolutionary movement. It was instead a doctrine first articulated by Judas, which found a fertile soil in the sufferings of the peasantry of Judea and Galilee. It gave origin to a popular movement that continued for more than a century with various organized expressions at different moments. In recognition of its doctrinal nucleus as an interpretation of the traditions of Israel Josephus reluctantly admits its existence alongside the three philosophies that he considers legitimate. Israel was in its origins, if our reading of the matter is correct, a libertarian movement of peasants who denied the lordship of any human king. Judas looks like a legitimate heir of this tradition in a pure form. Historically speaking, this fourth philosophy was the most legitimate philosophy of the four that vied for the loyalties of the Palestinian population in the first century C.E.

The Popular Movement in Israel

It is our hypothesis that during the years 6–135 C.E. we should understand the many conflicts that took place as so many expressions of a popular movement that was never able to articulate itself behind a "vanguard" until the last years, when Simon bar Cosiba (= bar Cochba) directed it to an open conflict with the Roman legions. We take the following as expressions of this movement: Judas the Galilean, John the Baptist and his followers, Jesus of Nazareth and his followers, Theudas, the Sicarii of the 50s, the various revolutionary factions during the First War with Rome (66–74 C.E.), and the popular rebellion led by Simon, which ended in the Second (and last) War with Rome (132–35 C.E.).

We know nothing about the rebellion of Judas in 6 C.E. except what Josephus says about his deep love of freedom and his conviction that freedom ought to be defended by the force of arms, whether one triumphed or died in the effort, in which case one would at least earn honor and fame (*timen kai kleos, Ant.* 18§5). It is likely that he perished in combat, but we do not have a witness to that effect.

A movement arose around a teacher from Nazareth named Jesus about the year 30 C.E.. We know of him by means of the four gospels, which were written by followers interested in Jesus no longer as a popular teacher and leader, but as the founder of a new way toward God and salvation open to all, both Jewish and non-Jewish. In spite of the tendentiousness of our sources of information, it is possible to read the behavior of the movement in Galilee and later in Judea as an expression of the popular movement that so agitated the Palestinian scene during those years.

The Christian gospels also testify to the existence of a prophet John and his followers at this same time. Judging by the Christian witness to John, he was also part of this broad popular movement in Palestine. The Essenes withdrew to the desert to establish a priestly community as an alternative to the corrupt priesthood of Jerusalem. John's withdrawal with his followers to the desert was a prophetic withdrawal in the spirit of Elijah. From his prophetic pulpit in the desert he lashed out at the leaders of Jewish society. Whether he called for the overthrow of the Herods in the spirit of Samuel and Elisha we do not know; our sources are interested rather in John's purported endorsement of Jesus as the expected one foretold by the prophets of old. We cannot be sure of this endorsement because of the bias of our sources, but it is worthy of credence that Jesus showed his support for John's preaching by letting himself be baptized as a sign of repentance and renewal. It is also likely that John's life was ended by Herod Antipas. This ending makes it likely that his preaching had important political tones directed, as Jesus' teaching was, primarily at the local authorities (rather than at the Romans themselves).

When we read the Christian gospels in light of our knowledge of the popular movement some key elements emerge: First, Jesus and his followers saw the principal antagonist to the kingdom of God in the Jerusalem Temple, and interpreted the Pharisaic movement in Galilee as their support group locally. As for his relation to Judas's teaching, the central theme of Jesus' teaching was that God is king and that God's kingdom may be expected as a new and perfect society. He differed from Judas in that he did not see the Romans' oppression as the most intolerable but rather that of the religious Jews. In keeping with this analysis, the Jesus movement did not attack the Roman presence but staged a symbolic attack on the Temple, followed by several days of polemics with the priests and scribes who ruled there until they had Jesus removed by force.

Like Judas, Jesus was perceived primarily as a teacher (a philosopher, in the spirit of Cynic and Stoic popular teachers of the age). As such he made the Pharisees a prime target of his attacks on the ideological structures of Galilean society. Their emphasis on obedience to the law of God made them in effect the justifiers of the Temple oppression. (This debate between Jesus and the Galilean Pharisees is "contaminated" in our sources by the ongoing debates between the Christian churches and the synagogues in the cities of Syria, Asia, and Achaea a generation later. Nevertheless, it seems coherent with what we know of Jesus in Galilee that some of this debate goes back to him and his contemporaries.)

Second, the strategy of the Jesus movement was to attack on the ideological plane in an effort to delegitimize the domination that found its support in the law of God. "The Sabbath was made for humans, and not humans for the Sabbath." God is a generous Father more than a frightful judge. The kingdom is like a landholder who pays all his workers their full daily wage because they need it, even those who did not do the work to "deserve" it (Matt. 20:1-15). If this is the nature of the God of Israel, God cannot be concerned about the fulfillment of religious duties, but rather about those matters that sustain life. Compared with Judas, Jesus' popular strategy resembles that of Gramsci against Lenin. Where Judas (apparently) sought power in order to transform the conditions of life for the people, Jesus sought to take away the basis of the consensus through which it was possible for the Temple to oppress the people. Once this was accomplished, once an alternative consensus had been composed at the base of society, the question of power could be undertaken in a new fashion.

Third, Jesus sought in the present alien society to create a small community that would organize itself along the lines of brother- and sisterhood that characterize God's kingdom. Neither wealth nor family connections counted as privileges in this community, just the willingness to be fully at the disposal of the "brothers and sisters." The movement required of its followers a break with society, the abandonment of both wealth and family. For Jesus the question of power was not primary in the direction he tried to give to the popular movement. Power flowed from the service to those at the base rather than in a hierarchical manner. In Jesus' teaching God is like a landlord who exposes his envoys, and even his own son, to the abuse of power from persons smaller than he and who do not understand or do not wish to understand the ultimate purposes of the kingdom (Mark 12:1-12).

Finally, the popular movement as Jesus conceived it was nationalistic, as it had to be under the conditions of imperialism, but with a nationalism open to others (conceived also as oppressed). It is not by accident that he is quoted during the critical assault on the Temple as using the words of Jeremiah and Isaiah ("Trito-Isaiah"), "My house shall be called a house of prayer for all nations" (Isa. 56:7) "but you have made it a den of thieves" (Jer. 7:11). Jeremiah also criticized the Temple and its personnel, and concluded that the people should recognize the Babylonian presence as the will of God (Jer. 25:1-10). Facing the *Gola* with its pretensions of racial purity, some of the popular prophets we know as Trito-Isaiah advocated a generous and open view of God's salvation. Jesus sought to move the popular movement in Galilee and Judea into this broad line, nationalist but not exclusive.

The Jesus movement survived his death at the hands of a coalition of Jewish and Roman authorities. It became a defensive movement that challenged the dominant society by its life-style. In Jerusalem there was an attempt to adopt a communitarian style in a resident community of foreigners (Galileans, Cypriots, Syrians, and others; Acts 2:42-47). But it became increasingly sectarian, seeing itself against the nation, us against them, followers of Jesus against "the Jews." At least part of the movement in the city heightened Jesus' critique of the Temple into an outright attack on its legitimacy in God's eyes, represented by Luke in Stephen's sermon (Acts 7). The authorities repelled the challenge by stoning Stephen. Apparently, Jesus' more radical followers (identified by Luke as "Hellenists") fled Jerusalem. Nevertheless, the repression continued, and King Herod Agrippa I had James, the son of Zebedee, killed. Later the high priest Ananus had the other James, the brother of Jesus, killed in 62 C.E. The death of this key leader forced the movement out of Israel, thus making it lose its contact with the popular movement in Galilee. The openness of their nationalism allowed them to redefine themselves and to survive in the cities of the empire, where they became "churches" (religious associations) and ceased to be part of the history of Israel.

According to Josephus (*Ant.* 20§97ff.), in the times of the procurator Cuspius Fadus (44–46 C.E.) a certain Theudas arose who claimed to be a prophet and who managed a popular following to "part the Jordan." His movement ended abruptly when the procurator, seeing his authority threatened, had Theudas beheaded and his head brought to Jerusalem.

During the following years there were several incidents in which the population, both urban and rural, protested the abuses of power committed by the authorities. Tiberius Alexander, procurator from 46 to 48, sentenced and crucified James and Simon, sons of Judas the Galilean, although Josephus does not inform us about their revolutionary activities (*Ant.* 20§102).

Early during the government of Felix (52–60 C.E.) the popular movement took a new form in the actions of a group known as the Sicarii. These revolutionaries assassinated persons considered to be enemies of the people in the midst of crowds of pilgrims during the festivals. Their pattern was to wear a dagger under their clothes, to kill their victim suddenly, and then to disappear in the crowd (*J.W.* 2§254–56). The first victim of this activity was the high priest Jonathan, which is a significant indication of how the Sicarii perceived the dominant Jewish stratum. The tactic would not have worked against the Romans anyway, for they did not mix with the local population in the festive crowds. The Sicarii reappeared later during the war, so that it is clear that they were an organized group (and not a few isolated assassins).

The insurrection that broke out as war against Rome in 66 C.E. seems to have arisen more or less spontaneously in several places as a popular reaction to a series of abuses. Among these a decision stands out by the emperor Nero ruling in favor of the Greeks in a dispute involving a synagogue's access to the street in Caesarea. Among the leaders of the insurrection, Josephus lists the five groups previously mentioned: Sicarii, Zealots, Idumeans, and followers of John of Gischala and Simon bar Giora. Toward the beginning of the insurrection the authorities in Jerusalem made an effort to direct and channel popular anger. Ananus the high priest assumed the direction of a provisional government. It was this government that named Josephus, a young priest affiliated to the Pharisees, to head the military actions in Galilee, where the hostilities were most serious. Their intention seems to have been both to force reparations for the offenses of the Romans against the Jewish population and also to prevent the revolutionary movement from taking a radical course against the priests themselves. During the course of a year there were several battles, but then the rebel forces were trapped in Jotpata, a town in the heart of the Galilean hills. Jotpata fell in the summer of 67 C.E. and almost all the defenders lost their lives, some by their own hand. Josephus, the general, was taken prisoner.

The scenario changed, with the center of action moving to Jerusalem. The rebels took the city, and for the following years it was the scene of the most violent actions. Menahem, a descendent of Judas the Galilean, led a victorious assault on Herod's palace in the city, but he then fell, assassinated by Eleazar, a leader of the priestly band, forcing his followers to withdraw from the city and take refuge in the spectacular hilltop fort Massada, where they were able to survive until the end of the war. In 67 C.E. the Zealots appealed to the Idumeans to assist the rebels, arguing that the provisional government was making an arrangement with the Romans, which may have been true. The high priest was assassinated in the "liberated" city, and a new high priest was chosen "democratically" by lots. The chosen one was a certain Phani, apparently a peasant (*J.W.* 4§155ff.). This is a clear illustration of the social character of the struggle of the Zealots, whose places of origin appear to have been the villages of Judea.

The Sicarii played a major role during the first phase of the struggle over Jerusalem, among whom Josephus mentions a certain Menahem. It was they who burned down the house of Ananus the high priest, and the building of the public archives where the debts of the population were recorded and filed away (*J.W.* 2§427). After the murder of Menahem, they withdrew from the city and resisted in Massada until 74 C.E.

Later in the battle to defend Jerusalem John of Gischala (a town in the interior of Galilee) and Simon bar Giora (from Gerasa in Transjordan) emerged as major leaders. Simon in particular was a radical revolutionary with a program of elimination of all wealth and other signs of inequality. He was, in addition, a disciplined man whose military leadership in the defense of the city proved quite effective. When Titus finally captured the city in 70 C.E. he took both John and Simon captives to exhibit them in the public triumphal ceremony in Rome.

With the fall and destruction of Jerusalem the rebellion lost all hope of success. The popular revolutionaries had been able to pull together a great mass of people and to wage of war on a large scale. Almost the whole of the

Jewish population of Palestine found itself forced to join the rebellion, which was led by the popular forces. The main base of these forces was the peasantry, from whom came the Zealots, the Sicarii, and the forces of John of Gischala and Simon bar Giora, but there were also popular forces from cities like Ceasarea and Gerasa.

In Jerusalem they had the typical problem for a revolutionary movement, simultaneously having to fight the elitist groups in the nation to carry through a revolutionary program and also to organize and carry out the defense against the imperial armies. The situation was further complicated by fights among the revolutionaries for the main positions in the movement, but the decisive element in the defeat of the movement was the incomparably superior military force of the Romans, who in the end rolled over all the opposition.

In some places it was possible to maintain small foci of resistance for a few more years after the fall of Jerusalem. The last outpost to fall was Massada, where the Sicarii had ensconced themselves. They died in a justly celebrated collective suicide in the face of their desperate situation in 74 C.E.

This was still not the end. The lot of the peasantry continued to be intolerable. The destruction of the Temple and of Jerusalem made it difficult to resurrect a project along the lines of the Deuteronomists and the Maccabees. The revolution that exploded in 132 C.E. had as its axis the agrarian reform, as can be seen from the documents that the revolutionaries left in the caves of Murabba'at and Nahal Hever.

This took place during the government of Emperor Hadrian. He had passed through Palestine in 130 C.E. leaving several Hellenistic monuments in cities like Caesarea and Tiberias. It was possibly at this time that he launched a project to found a Roman city called Aelia Capitolina on the location where Jerusalem had existed, access to which would be forbidden for Jews.

Unfortunately, we know very little about the revolutionary movement headed by Simon bar Cosiba. It seems to have been a movement of great dimensions, comparable in scope to the first revolution of 66–74 C.E., but in this case the unquestioned leader was one, Simon. Once in power he implemented important legal reforms, especially related to agrarian matters. His principal advisor was the famous rabbi Akiba, who called him the "Star of David," a Messianic title (from Num. 24:17). Simon avoided open confrontations with the Roman troops, limiting his military actions to forays of harassment. His forces found refuge in caves, out of which they carried on their struggle. Hadrian found it necessary to send one of his best generals, Julius Severus, to squelch the rebellion. Severus managed to corral Simon in the town of Bethar near Jerusalem, which fell to the Romans in 135 C.E. All that remained was to eliminate operations in the caves to end the resistance.

The measures the Romans took eliminated the remainder of the experiment Israel. Hellenistic cities dominated the land, the religious and cultural centers of Israel were destroyed, and the cultural identity of the peasants of the lands was eventually eliminated.

The Jamnia Epilogue

Before the battle of Jerusalem, in 67 C.E., a famous rabbi (teacher of law and Scripture) named Johanan ben Zakkai withdrew from the city. He obtained permission from the Romans to establish at Jamnia, in the territory that had been Philistia, a *bet din*, a house of study and court of law. There, under the leadership of Johanan, the foundations were laid for the rabbinic Judaism that would give identity for many centuries to Jewish people dispersed in the urban centers of the world. To be a Jew ceased to mean to belong to the peasant people Israel. It meant belonging to a community that lived in accord with the laws and customs that God gave to Moses and that the rabbis interpreted so they might serve as rules for the conduct of life in the urban centers of the whole world.

Bibliography

It is impossible to acknowledge the enormous debt that the author owes to a multitude of scholars in biblical studies and related fields. Nor would it serve the reader of this small history to append a large bibliography. But a basic honesty and gratitude require some indication of those scholars whose works undergird this reading in its more debatable points.

If I were to point to only one biblical critic whose work was fundamental for the present book, he would be the meticulous Leipzig scholar Albrecht Alt (1883–1956), who wrote essays on every period of biblical history. Alt followed what he called the "territorial method," pursuing the administrative arrangement of each period and always asking about the divisions of the territory of Palestine under every ruler. This is not yet a history of the life of the common people, but Alt's insistence on the geography of the governments and empires gave his work an impressive concreteness. His scholarly work was published in scientific journals and was gathered toward the end of his life in two volumes: Albrecht Alt, *Kleine Schriften zur Geschichte des Volkes Israel* Munich: C. H. Beck, 1953. After Alt's death in 1956, Martin Noth gathered a third volume of Alt's work, which was incorporated into the second edition of this work published in 1959. The many valuable studies within this collection have assisted me very much for all of the periods of the history of Israel.

One of the most complicated matters in the history of any of the peoples of antiquity is that of chronology. After many struggles with the puzzles that the chronology of Israel presents to the scholar, I decided that it would not be possible to assume responsibility for resolving this complicated issue. I decided for the period of the monarchy

(931–586 B.C.E.), where there are texts but their reconciliation and interpretation is sorely disputed, to rely strictly on De Vries and thus to avoid arbitrary and possibly capricious decisions. De Vries's interpretation can be found in: Simon J. De Vries, "Chronology of the Old Testament," in *Interpreter's Dictionary of the Bible*. Nashville: Abingdon, 1962, 1:580–99.

For the origins of Israel the work of Norman K. Gottwald has been indispensable, not just for historical details but also for the reading from the perspective of the poor. The primary book is Norman K. Gottwald, *The Tribes of Yahweh: A Sociology of the Religion of Liberated Israel, 1250–1050 B.C.E.* Maryknoll, N.Y.: Orbis, 1979.

For the crucial problem of the critical evaluation of the Deuteronomistic and Chronistic histories I have relied mainly on the following:

Martin Noth. *Überlieferungsgeschichtliche Studien*. Tübingen, 1957 (the original edition was from 1943). This is the basic work on which all later work relies.

Richard Elliott Friedman. *The Exile and biblical Narrative: The Formation of the Deuteronomistic and Priestly Works*. Chico, California: Scholars Press, 1981.

A.D.H. Mayes. *The Story of Israel between Settlement and Exile: A Redactional Study of the Deuteronomistic History.* London: SCM Press, 1983. I know the work of Manfred Weippert on the historical writing that lies behind 1 Kings 22 to 2 Kings 17 only through Mayes's report on pp. 120–22.

For the interpretation of the social dynamics of the Persian period I have found to be especially useful the works of Hanson and Petersen:

Paul D. Hanson. *The Dawn of Apocalyptic: The Historical and Sociological Roots of Jewish Apocalyptic Eschatology.* Philadelphia: Fortress, 1975

David L. Petersen. *Late Israelite Prophecy: Studies in Deutero-Prophetic Literature and in Chronicles*. Chico: Scholars Press, 1977.

Other works that have been important for various periods are:

Julio C. Trebolle Barrera. *Salomón y Jeroboán: Historia de la recensión y redacción de I Reyes 2–12; 14*. Salamanca: Universidad Pontificia, 1980.

Frank S. Frick. *The Formation of the State in Ancient Israel.* Decatur, Georgia: Almond, 1985.

Martin Hengel. *Judaism and Hellenism*. 2 volumes. Philadelphia: Fortress, 1974.

David C. Hopkins. *The Highlands of Canaan: Agricultural Life in the Early Iron Age*. Decatur, Georgia: Almond, 1985.

H. Jagersma. *A History of Israel from Alexander the Great to Bar Kochba*. Philadelphia: Fortress, 1986.

Burton L. Mack. *Wisdom and the Hebrew Epic: Ben Sira's Hymn in Praise of the Fathers*. Chicago: University of Chicago Press, 1985.

B. Mazar. "The Tobiads," in *Israel Exploration Journal*, 7 (1957): 137–45; 229–38.

B. Oded. "The Historical Background of the Syro-Ephraimite War Reconsidered," in *Catholic Biblical Quarterly* 34 (1972): 153–65.

David M. Rhoads. *Israel in Revolution, 6–74* C.E. Philadelphia: Fortress, 1976.

For the understanding of the Asiatic or tributary mode of production I have found helpful, in addition to the writings of Karl Marx, the anthology by Roger Bartra (ed.), *El modo de producción asiático*. Mexico: Era, 1969.

Name and Subject Index

Scripture Index

Apocrypha